ADVANCES

BUS
STO

MAKING ADVANCES

What you can do about sexual harassment at work

by Liz Curtis

BBC BOOKS

This book is published to accompany the Continuing Education television
series entitled *Making Advances* which was first broadcast in 1993.
The independent production company was Vanson Wardle Productions.

Published by BBC Books,
a division of BBC Enterprises Limited,
Woodlands, 80 Wood Lane, London W12 0TT

First published 1993

ISBN 0 563 36960 4

Designed by Gwyn Lewis
Set in Gill Sans and Galliard by Goodfellow & Egan Limited, Cambridge

Printed and bound in Great Britain by Clays Ltd, St Ives plc
Cover printed by Clays Ltd, St Ives plc

Contents

AUTHOR'S NOTE

Some of the stories in this book are very offensive. I felt they should be included because similar things will have happened to other women, and they may draw comfort from the fact that they are not alone.

Sexual harassment can be very painful. Many of the women who have taken legal action do not wish to be reminded of their experience, nor to have any more publicity. For that reason, except where cases have a particular legal significance, I have not used their full names. Also, I have changed the names of most of the people who gave their stories directly to me or to my co-researchers, Lin Solomon and Tony Wardle.

PUBLISHER'S NOTE

Acknowledgements

This book could not have been written without the help of a great many people.

Deep thanks are first of all due to the many women, and the handful of men, whose stories, often painful, are the heart of the book.

Very important are the people with special knowledge of this subject who gave me their time. They include Irene Hamilton of City Centre, Debbi King of Hillingdon Legal Resource Centre, Vicki Merchant and Jane Johnson of the National Harassment Network, Dr Gillian Mezey of St George's Hospital Medical School, Sinead Mulhern of the Equal Opportunities Commission for Northern Ireland, and Michael Rubenstein. I also drew on the written work of many people, including lawyer Amanda Croxon and educationalist Carrie Herbert, as well as others who are cited in the references.

Many trade unionists have given invaluable help, including Pauline Bean of the GMB, Sally Gilbert of the NUJ, Amor Jones of MSF, Pam Monk of BIFU, Jo Morris of the TUC, and Maureen O'Mara of Unison.

Countless friends and acquaintances have contributed ideas, information and contacts, among them Melissa Benn, Susy Bond, Aude Catala, Anne Clarke, Tessa Coombs, Roisin Duffy, Linda Etchart, Lesley Exton, Rob Good, Ronald Grant, Maggie Hay, Bryony Hegarty, Virginia Heywood, Annie Janowitz, Mike Jempson, Pat Kahn, Pat Larkin-Coyle, Sarah Lewthwaite, John Lloyd, Pauline Matthews, Lucy Micklethwait, Joanne O'Brien, Frank O'Neill, David Pallister, Joyce Pratt, Aly Renwick, Fiona Rivers, Colin Robertson, Liz Rodgers, Jacqueline Schaebbicke,

Susan Schonfield, Lesley van Sleyke, Martin Smith, Roger Smith, Ruth Taillon, Mike Tomlinson, and Jane Winter.

The librarians of Hammersmith Reference Library and the staff of Bush Books were brilliant as usual. The staff of the various specialist organisations mentioned were unfailingly helpful – please forgive me for not mentioning everyone by name! Mary Honan of the Employment Equality Agency in Dublin kindly saw me at short notice.

I must thank Yvette Vanson and Tony Wardle of Vanson Wardle Productions for involving me in their television series on sexual harassment at work. Also at Vanson Wardle, thanks to researcher Lin Solomon, who shared her work with me, and to Ishia Bennison, Lavinia Glynn-Jones, Veronica Harris, Caroline Hodgson, and Val Howard.

At the BBC, thanks to Suzanne Webber, my commissioning editor, and to her assistant Khadija Manjlai, who was ever helpful. Thanks, too, to Chris Lent, commissioning editor of the series, and the production team on the book, who include Caroline Plaisted at the BBC.

Thanks, too, to Alex Kemp for giving me a massage when I really needed it, and to my new neighbours for being there (well, on and off).

To everyone who wanted to stay 'off the record', and to anyone I've forgotten – many thanks to you, too!

Finally, a giant 'thank you' to Faith Evans, my agent, for her vital support at all stages of the project.

And the usual disclaimer – none of the above have any responsibility for the contents of the book. (But I hope they like it!)

Liz Curtis
April 1993

Foreword

Sexual harassment blights the lives of many women. For some it is a minor unpleasantness – a stranger's clammy hand on your knee at the cinema, leers and wolf-whistles from groups of men in the street. For others it becomes a nightmare – working for years with a boss who tries to grope you whenever you're alone with him, or with male colleagues who torment you till you leave your job.

For many of us the problem is made worse because we feel that we are on our own. We are ashamed to discuss it. We feel that in some obscure way we have 'brought it on ourselves'. And we don't know how to begin dealing with it.

This handbook aims to help us deal with sexual harassment first by showing that we are not alone. Many women, in many walks of life, have suffered, and many have taken action. The book explains, too, that sexual harassment is not 'our fault' – rather, it is a social problem.

It goes on to suggest practical ways of tackling the problem. If that is your main interest, you can jump straight to Chapter Three.

There are various things we can do. We might confront the harasser alone, or enlist the help of friends and colleagues. We might use the procedures provided by managements and unions, or get in touch with specialist organisations. In the last resort, we might take legal action against employers or harassers.

Sexual harassment at work is very often directed by senior people against juniors, who may find it hard to fight back. So there is no easy recipe for dealing with it.

But things *are* changing. Governments are beginning to make

3

laws against sexual harassment. Trade unions and companies are developing policies and procedures to deal with it. Pressure groups are lobbying against it. And above all, women the world over are standing up and saying, 'No!'

Kiyomi Kikuchi, a twenty-five-year-old Japanese woman, sued her boss for sexual harassment, then demanded that he apologise through national newspapers. She made her name public – the first Japanese woman alleging sexual harassment to do so. She wanted, she said, 'to offer encouragement to women who are enduring sexual harassment in silence.'[1]

ONE

What is sexual harassment?

> *He wangled it so that he was alone in a car with me. He was the producer and I was a junior member of the production team. He suggested he could help me in my career. When we got back to the hotel – we were filming on location – he jumped into the lift behind me and proceeded to kiss me, and wanted to ... He's the foulest man. He doesn't wash. He smells awful. I was positively revolted by this and I was so shocked. I ran to my room and had such a hot shower. I just felt totally dirty and – yuk!*

That was only the start of Sandra's problems. After she rejected the producer's advances, she found herself picked on and bullied by other members of the team. Eventually she decided she had suffered enough, and changed to a different job.

Sandra's story is typical. Far from being the joke that many people think it is, sexual harassment can cause great misery and change the course of people's lives.

EMOTIONAL DAMAGE

Psychiatrist Dr Gillian Mezey often sees women who are taking legal action over sexual harassment. She assesses the psychological damage done to them, to help them claim compensation for injury to feelings. She explains:

> *The women feel tense, anxious and frightened. They feel very vulnerable and may stay away from work. Their self-confidence*

and self-esteem are very significantly affected by the way they are treated at work as a sexual object, simply valued for their sexuality and their femininity, rather than as a colleague or a worker.

'They become tearful and unable to sleep. They may have nightmares, often related to the harassment. They lose interest in eating and in socialising. Often it very badly affects their relationships at home with the family. They feel unsafe even with their partner. They lose interest in looking after the home and playing with the children.

99

These symptoms, Dr Mezey explains, are similar to those experienced by rape victims and survivors of major disasters.

Rosanna was constantly harassed by two male colleagues when she was employed by a glazing company. After being sacked, she went to a tribunal and won £5,000 and a formal letter of apology.

She recalled: 'My marriage suffered terribly throughout the whole affair. I hadn't told my husband what had been happening at work. I just thought he wouldn't have been able to do anything. He might even have wanted to go down there and hit them.'

Nurses and other health service workers, questioned by their trade union, described their experience of sexual harassment:

* 'I lost trust in men around me.'

* 'I was afraid to go to work.'

* 'It kept me awake at night . . . I'd dread him being at work.'

* 'It made me feel worthless, ashamed.'[2]

INTENSELY HUMILIATING

Even seemingly minor incidents can have serious effects. What women find particularly distressing is when they come to work as workers, and find they are being treated merely as sexual objects, which undermines their identity and hence their confidence.

Sally, a high-powered advertising director for a financial magazine, felt intensely humiliated when her boss came up behind her and stroked her bottom while she was giving instructions to her sales staff. 'It was not a sexual gesture. It was about control, belittling me in front of my staff.'

After a succession of incidents, which left her anxious, withdrawn and unconfident, she gave in her notice and then took legal action. The company settled out of court for £25,000 damages and legal costs.

June was working as a cleaner for an agency. She recalls: 'I went into this office block and the manager said, "You don't need to work. Come with me." He took me into the lift and started hugging and kissing me. I just walked straight out of the job.'

A similar incident happened to June in another firm, leaving her feeling both vulnerable and angry. 'Men think that if they are paying you to clean, you will be equally willing to be paid to have sex. They deny you the dignity of work.'

BLACK AND ASIAN WOMEN

For black and Asian women the problem can be particularly severe, because sexual harassment is compounded by racism. They may find they are on the receiving end of particularly offensive insults, and may have even greater difficulties than white women trying to sort out such problems. They may find that white supervisors side with white harassers, or that managers simply find problems which combine sexism and racism too 'messy' to deal with.

Amina, an electronics engineer, was persistently harassed by her white manager. He was always touching her and saying things like, 'Come with me and I'll make a woman of you.'

She told him not to do it, and he started threatening to sack her and making racial comments such as, 'I don't want the fucking Paki bastard in here.'

A new manager arrived and behaved the same way as the first one. He repeatedly asked her out, pressed himself against her and made sexual remarks. When she told him not to, he got nasty.

Amina became distressed and lost weight. She reported the matter to personnel and was moved to another section. The second manager sent her abusive and disgusting notes. Eventually she reported this to management, and the following day she was called in, made redundant and seen off the premises.

One of those who has turned for help to the Commission for Racial Equality was a young Muslim woman who was intimidated by workmates. They told her they would have to send her on a special course to teach her about sex.[3]

Ms C was a full-time trade union official. A fellow official told her he liked Asian women's bodies and suggested they start a relationship. When she refused, he persecuted her. He shouted at her in front of colleagues, overloaded her with work, and removed her secretarial assistance.

The union eventually settled out of court, but Ms C felt forced to leave the job, which she loved.

UNDERMINING WOMEN

In general, where work is concerned, women have a harder time than men. They are paid less, they have lower status jobs, and they often carry the main burden of work at home as well.

The overall effect of sexual harassment is to keep them in second place, and to undermine their moves towards equality.

Because of sexual harassment, they can find themselves sacked or forced to resign. They may become unconfident and hence less able to work on an equal footing with men. They may withdraw from male-dominated workplaces altogether, or even, in extreme cases, retire completely to the home.

Confronting sexual harassment is, therefore, part of the wider battle to improve the position of women in society.

Susan is a freelance accountant. She was sexually harassed by her boss for two years when she was in her early twenties. Now, twenty years later, she says, 'It made me very suspicious of men. I only work for women now.'

WHERE SEXUAL HARASSMENT HAPPENS: IN THE COMMONS AND ON THE BUSES

Sexual harassment happens everywhere: in debates at the House of Commons, in lecture halls and hospital wards, in offices, and on the factory floor.

✱ *The House of Lords:* A prominent peer is known to office staff in the Houses of Parliament as MTF – 'Must Touch Flesh'.

✱ *The House of Commons:* Tory MP Teresa Gorman told a journalist: 'When Clare Short talked about the horrors of back-street abortion, there were comments like, "you should know, you old slag".'[4]
    Gorman herself was vilified by MPs because she was having hormone replacement therapy. They shouted, 'Are you a man or a woman?' and 'Show us your birth certificate!'[5]

✱ *The law:* 'Sexual harassment is still rife in the legal profession,' says barrister Helena Kennedy. 'I know several women who have experienced it from male lawyers but felt if they had complained it would have blighted their careers. Twenty years ago I had to deal with senior lawyers who kept making comments full of sexual innuendo and who tried to touch me – patting me on the behind, that kind of thing.'[6]

✱ *Police:* A Home Office report revealed that nearly all policewomen have experienced sexual harassment from policemen, and uniformed patrol officers were most likely to be harassed. Six per cent of policewomen had experienced serious sexual assaults by policemen, and ten per cent had considered leaving the force because of sexual harassment.[7]

✱ *Hospitals:* A woman doctor described in the British Medical Journal how a senior colleague had clutched her buttocks and squeezed, then casually walked away. She recalled other men: 'A registrar who was constantly wolf-whistling staff down corridors, flicking up our skirts, bringing his sexual exploits into the conversation, brushing against nurses' bodies, and entering female house officers' rooms offering to go to bed with them . . . The teachers who showed pornographic pin-ups in surgery and gynaecology lectures . . . A forensic pathologist who gloats and jokes over slides of beaten, dead and raped women.'[8]

* *Office workers:* A survey in 1991 by the employment agency Alfred Marks found that eighty-eight per cent of their clients had observed sexual harassment towards themselves or others.

* *Bus workers:* A survey by London Buses Ltd found that over fifty per cent of women surveyed had substantial experience of harassment.

* *Students:* A survey by the National Union of Students found that ninety-five per cent of students surveyed had suffered some form of sexual harassment.

* *Town hall staff:* A survey by the Liverpool branch of NALGO – the union covering white-collar council staff – found that fifty-five per cent of women surveyed had experienced sexual harassment in their present or previous jobs.

EVERYONE HAS A STORY

Virtually every woman has a story – and not just 'straight' women. Lesbians and gay men may be tormented on account of their sexual orientation. Jokes and teasing are common, but abuse, threats and assault also occur.

A gay man told a health service union survey that when he was harassed, it took the form of 'anonymous letters, copies of anti-gay newspapers pinned up or sent to me'.

The organisation Lesbian Employment Rights says in a report: 'Male sexual harassment of women does not restrict itself to heterosexual women. Lesbians who are perceived as attractive, according to conventional standards of feminine beauty, seem to pose a particular challenge. Lesbians who are not considered attractive are subject to vicious insults and harassment.'[9]

Even 'straight' men sometimes suffer – when, for example, a man finds himself out-numbered by women, or in the rare situations where a woman has considerable power and authority over a man.

Paul, a writer, remembered: 'When I was a young freelance journalist, the editor of a woman's magazine promised me regular work if I would go to bed with her. She was horrible! I refused, and never worked for her again.'

Paul's experience is very unusual, mainly because women seldom have so much power. Because the overwhelming majority of sufferers from sexual harassment are women, this handbook will refer to them as female.

A London Buses survey found that ninety-six per cent of men at East London Garages had *never* been subjected to 'uninvited and deliberate touching of intimate parts of the body', compared to forty per cent of women.

ALL AREAS OF LIFE

Sexual harassment affects all kinds of women, in all areas of life. It can affect us in the street, on public transport, in museums and cinemas, at the optician and dentist, at work, and even at home.

Julie, an eighteen-year-old clerk, was pestered every day for weeks as she travelled to work on the London underground. Gary, a twenty-five-year-old City analyst, described pornographic acts he wanted to carry out with her, made rude gestures with his tongue, and groped her on a crowded platform. Eventually Julie pointed him out to police, and he was fined £500 with £430 costs for indecent assault.

Some years ago performance artist Laurie Anderson travelled American cities with a Polaroid camera. Whenever a man wolf-whistled or cat-called, she snapped the shutter. Men got angry and tried to take the camera from her. She collected hundreds of portraits, wrote the date, time and place on each, and put them up in an art gallery.[10]

At work, women have problems not only with bosses and colleagues, but also from the public. This is especially true for people such as nurses, waitresses and home helps.

More than seventy per cent of nurses surveyed by researchers at the University of Plymouth had experienced sexual harassment, mostly from patients but also from colleagues, doctors and visitors.[11]

Marie, a waitress in a London restaurant, says, 'I can deal with sexual harassment from other staff, but I have real problems with some of the customers, especially foreign businessmen and tourists. You can't be rude because they are customers.

'I had one group of tourists – they wanted me to say I would go out with one of them. They tried to get me to introduce them to three young ladies sitting at another table and proceeded to annoy them, so they soon left. They asked me if I had any friends that they might like, and what was I doing afterwards.

'It makes you feel really uncomfortable, because you don't want to go back to that table, and you know that every time you walk past them they're looking you up and down.'

'Cathy, a home help and shop steward, says: 'Some women laugh it off or make a joke, as it is elderly men we work with. I had problems which involved physical contact by a client, an elderly man, but it wasn't funny. It got so bad that I was ill because of it and I had to get a transfer.'[12]

FIGHTING BACK

Sexual harassment is a very old problem, but it wasn't till the 1970s that it was given a name. Before that, women tended to regard it as unpleasant but inevitable. Then they began fighting back.

The 1960s and 1970s were decades of struggle throughout the world. In Africa, Asia and Latin America, people fought to throw off the shackles of colonialism. In the United States, black people got together to demand equal rights with whites and an end to segregation. In Northern Ireland, too, Catholics demanded civil rights.

Soon white Western women joined the fray, demanding equality with men and reviving a movement that had been asleep since the end of World War One.

Young women of the sixties' counter-culture rebelled against the sexism of their 'comrades', who expected them to make the tea and provide an easy lay. They protested against stereotyping and, in one instance, rushed the stage at the Miss World final in London in 1970 amid huge publicity. Next year gay liberationists were there too, dressed up as 'Miss Laid' and 'Miss Used'.[13]

Women wrote:

> 66
>
> *We have been in the Miss World contest all our lives . . . judging ourselves as the judges judge us – living to please men – dividing other women up into safe friends and attractive rivals – graded, degraded, humiliated . . . we've seen through it . . .*[14]
>
> 99

Women demanded equal pay at work and equal sharing of chores at home. They demanded control of their bodies and the right to abortion. They protested against male violence against women, especially wife-battering and rape, and set up refuges and rape crisis centres. They also worked to recover their history, digging in obscure corners to reveal the story of earlier women's liberation movements and women's lives in the past, buried by the prejudice of male historians.

They were derided by the press as harridans and harpies, ugly creatures in dungarees.

In her path-breaking book, *The Female Eunuch*, published in 1970, Germaine Greer wrote: 'I'm sick of pretending eternal youth. I'm sick of belying my own intelligence, my own will, my own sex. I'm sick of peering at the world through false eyelashes, so everything I see is mixed with a shadow of bought hairs . . . I'm sick of pretending that some fatuous male's self-important pronouncements are the objects of my undivided attention . . .'[15]

Women became aware that one of the ways they were 'kept in their place' was by a thousand-and-one humiliations which they named 'sexual harassment'. The first surveys were done in the USA in 1976. The Working Women United Institute found that from fifty to seventy per cent of the women they questioned had experienced sexual harassment at some time in their working lives.

Of 9,000 women who replied to a questionnaire in *Redbook Magazine*, 8,100 said they had been sexually harassed.

In 1979 Catharine MacKinnon's pioneering book, *Sexual Harassment of Working Women*, was published in the USA.[16] She argued that sexual harassment was sex discrimination, and that therefore it was against the law, and women should be able to obtain redress through the courts.

Soon, campaigns against sexual harassment began in other countries. In Britain, organisations such as the National Council for Civil Liberties and the local government union NALGO took up the issue. Then in 1985 Women Against Sexual Harassment was founded, to publicise the problem and give practical help to people who were being harassed.

JEAN PORCELLI'S BREAKTHROUGH

In 1986 came a legal breakthrough when Jean Porcelli, a laboratory technician in a Scottish school who had been viciously harassed, won her case that her employers, Strathclyde Regional Council, had broken the Sex Discrimination Act 1975. **This was the first such decision in a British court, and paved the way for many other women to take cases under the Sex Discrimination Act.**

From the moment she arrived at the school, Jean Porcelli had been subjected to nightmare bullying by the two other laboratory technicians, men named Coles and Reid, who wanted her to leave the school. They concealed information from her; they threw her personal possessions out of her desk; they stored heavy things in a cupboard so high that she needed a ladder to reach them; they allowed swing doors to swing back into her face when she was carrying heavy apparatus and could not protect herself.

They also – and this was crucial to the court's decision – harassed her in ways that they would not have harassed a man.

Jean Porcelli told an industrial tribunal that Mr Coles began to stare at her and make suggestive remarks: 'He would, for example, pick up a screw nail and ask me if I would like a screw. Another example was when he picked up a glass rod holder – which is shaped like a penis – and asked if I had any use for it. On several occasions he opened the *Daily Record* at page three and commented on my physical appearance in comparison with that of the nude female depicted in the newspaper . . . It was his practice to come behind me and take me unawares so that when I turned round he would brush against me.'[17]

In the Porcelli case, Lord Emslie said that, 'sexual harassment is a particularly degrading and unacceptable form of treatment which it must have been the intention of Parliament to restrain'.

ANITA HILL

The Anita Hill case in the USA in 1991 brought sexual harassment to the forefront of people's consciousness internationally.

Anita Hill was a young, black law lecturer and devout Christian who had worked at the Equal Employment Opportunities Commission under another lawyer, also black, named Clarence Thomas. When Thomas was nominated by President George Bush to become a member of the Supreme Court, senate hearings were held – as is normal in the USA – to assess his suitability.

Thomas's opponents heard rumours that he had sexually harassed women, and senate staff questioned Anita Hill, who told them that Thomas had sexually harassed her. But at the senate hearings, the senators did not pay much attention to the charges – a fact which angered many women when the story became public.

Hill's allegations were leaked to the press, leading to an uproar, which persuaded Congress to hold special and public hearings. Both Hill and Thomas appeared and were cross-questioned, their testimonies broadcast on television across the USA and to countries around the world.

At the hearings:

66

Hill described a continuing pattern of verbal assault, especially the recounting of pornographic movies that featured rape, women being penetrated by animals, and large-breasted women. In one incidence of harassment, Thomas asked who had left a pubic hair on a Coke can . . . Mr Thomas talked about the size of his penis and his ability to give women pleasure through oral sex. These confidences were forced on Ms Hill in the workplace, in private, without witnesses . . . The verbal assaults humiliated Ms Hill and pushed her face in her sexual status . . . They put her in her place, which was under him; in the office; in the movie; in life – her life.

Andrea Dworkin[18]

At the hearings, Thomas claimed he was the victim of a 'high-tech lynching' and right-wing white male senators inflicted crass and hostile questioning on Anita Hill.

The senators did not accept Anita Hill's account, and confirmed Judge Clarence Thomas as a member of the Supreme Court. But in the wider world, many people believed Anita Hill.

For many black Americans, the hearings were a painful experience. They wondered if the issue was being so dramatically aired because the main figures were black. Writer Toni Morrison observed:

An accusation of such weight as sexual misconduct would probably have disqualified a white candidate on its face. Rather than any need for 'proof', the slightest possibility that it was publicly verifiable would have nullified the candidacy, forced the committee members to insist on another nominee rather than entertain the necessity for public debate on so loathsome a charge.

But in a racialized and race-conscious society, standards are changed, facts marginalized, repressed, and the willingness to air such charges, actually to debate them, outweighed the seemliness of a substantive hearing, because the actors were black.[19]

Anita Hill's story reverberated around the world, inflaming women with sympathetic anger and making at least some men start questioning themselves.

Perhaps what every man over thirty who has sat shiftily through the week's proceedings now needs is a way of dealing with accumulated guilt. A sexual harassment amnesty. The equiva-lent of one of those police skips for illegally owned guns where they could own up to the battery of double entendres, crude jokes, little touches, one-sided sexual conversations and insinuations which they have laid on women over most of their working lives.

Laurie Taylor, *The Times, 18 October 1991*

FREQUENT SCENARIOS

Some frequent scenarios of long-term sexual harassment are:

* The 'groping' boss, who demands sexual favours, often in return for promising to help with the woman's career, or under threat of undermining it.

   A seventeen-year-old girl from Portadown in Northern Ireland left her job after just two weeks because of sexual harassment by her boss. He frequently put his arm round her and once put his hand on her thigh. Then he subjected her to much more serious and offensive treatment, so that she fled in distress to the toilet and did not return to work next day. She went to an industrial tribunal and received £3,200 in compensation.

* The persecuting male group, who cannot handle the arrival of a woman in a previously male-dominated workplace, and respond by tormenting her.

   Adenike, a trainee painter and decorator still in her teens, went to work on a building site with twenty men. They tormented her for three years, touching her up, making disgusting remarks, showing her pornographic photographs and threatening physical attacks. One man even exposed himself. She suffered depression, went sick and eventually resigned. She took legal action and her employers, a north London council, settled by paying her £16,500 in damages and legal costs.

✱ The junior man or men who don't like being told what to do by a more senior woman, and give her a hard time.

'They say things behind your back, like "That woman needs a good screw."' Celia, a senior civil servant

The first woman director of *Spitting Image*, the satirical TV puppet show, found herself working with 120 men. She was greeted by a puppeteer who yelled, 'Hey, we got some pussy on the floor. How d'you feel about that, boys?'[20]

HARASSING JUNIORS

Although many women who are sexually harassed are young, older women too are affected. Nor do women need to be particularly beautiful or 'sexy' to attract harassment.

A harasser will usually target a woman who he thinks will be too frightened for her job to fight back. So he will often pick on someone junior. A 'groper' will often harass several women at the same time – though each may think she is the only one. Like all bullies, he will pick on people who seem weaker than himself.

But if the harassed person says 'no', and has the full support of colleagues, union and management, the chances are that the harasser or harassers will back off – unless they are foolish enough to risk their job or reputation.

Judge William Crawford, fifty-six years old, married and with a distinguished legal and sporting background, found himself in the glare of publicity after Suzanne, a court usher in her twenties and mother of two, complained that he had kissed her on both cheeks and put his hands on her waist. Judge Crawford made a written apology to Suzanne, which she accepted. But after other allegations of over-familiarity towards female court staff came to light, Judge Crawford was told to stay away from the courts while the matter was investigated.

FORMS OF HARASSMENT

There are many lists of what sexual harassment may include, and many general definitions. The shopworkers' union USDAW suggests it can involve:

* Sexual advances exercised by force

* Unnecessary and unwelcome non-accidental bodily contact and touching

* Sexual propositions

* Objectionable comments about one's appearance

* Degrading or abusive remarks and gestures, leering and staring

* Offensive pin-ups and sexual jokes

* Comments about personal sexual activity or preference.

The intention of the harasser or harassers is often not necessarily sexual – rather their aim may be to humiliate or torment a woman.

Sally, an executive, was awarded £25,000 after claiming harassment by her boss. She said: 'Sexual harassment is a very powerful label and much misunderstood. People think it's about sex – that had nothing to do with my case. It is really about power and using your gender to undermine your professional credibility and to diminish your authority.'[21]

Consequently a report compiled for the Equal Opportunities Commission for Northern Ireland says that it is important not to focus solely on sexual desire or interest. The other type of harassment, which is not strictly sexual but makes a woman's work environment unpleasant, may be more difficult for many women to cope with.[22]

Indeed, the courts have recognised that sexual harassment does not have to involve sexual desire or interest, but may also describe harassment that occurs simply because of a person's sex.

Of course there is no god-given definition of sexual harassment, and we can define it as we wish. If we want to use it to solve the very wide variety of real problems that occur, it seems wise to be flexible.

Marie, a waitress, says: 'For me, sexual harassment is whenever you are made to feel uncomfortable by a male because of your status as a woman.'

In fact, 'sexist harassment' might be a better term. But the term 'sexual harassment' is now so widely used that it would be difficult to change it.

THE OPPOSITE OF ROMANCE

Sexual harassment is unpleasant, unwanted and often repellent. It is the complete opposite of romance, and has nothing to do with flirtation. Many people meet their future partners at work, and flirting is a natural preliminary.

But drawing the line between flirtatious joking and harassment is difficult. The key must be: are the people on both sides genuinely enjoying it? If you are gritting your teeth and struggling to think up a witty riposte, then it's moving towards harassment. It may be sensible to put a stop to it now – if it goes on, it may get harder to handle.

The key to what is sexual harassment is what the person on the receiving end feels is unacceptable. If somebody's behaviour makes you uncomfortable or unhappy, it's harassment. All the 'experts' – lawyers, educationalists, psychiatrists – are now agreed on this.

What makes you unhappy may be different from what makes someone else unhappy. One person may be able to tolerate a level of joking, for instance, that another finds stressful. Further, behaviour you might accept from one person you might detest from another. For your partner to put his hand on you at home is one thing; for your boss to do it at work is quite another.

It doesn't matter what the man says his reasons are. Men frequently say 'she asked for it' or claim that women should be flattered by their attentions. They remain wilfully blind to their victim's feelings and dream up justifications for their behaviour.

Rosanna said: 'I had always been chatty and friendly in the office. Work can be dull if you haven't got a sense of humour. But they just took things too far. It was relentless.'

Rosanna won £5,000 compensation and a letter of apology after being harassed by two male colleagues.[23]

TOUCHING

Touching can be a difficult area. A senior man may feel free to touch a more junior woman's body. It may well be a paternalistic or proprietorial gesture, and may not have sexual connotations. But consciously or unconsciously, the man is demonstrating that the woman is of lower status, dependent, childlike. The woman may well resent being touched, or feel uncomfortable about it, but may feel unable to tell him to stop.

One way of deciding whether the touching is acceptable or not is to ask: Would I feel happy doing the same thing back to him? Would he feel comfortable if I did?

What the law says about touching:
'The fundamental principle, plain and incontestable, is that every person's body is inviolate . . . the effect is that everybody is protected not only against physical injury but against any form of physical molestation'. Lord Justice Goff[24]

Yvonne, a secretary in the House of Commons, says: 'My boss is always putting his hand on my arm. It makes me profoundly uncomfortable. He is a good employer in every other respect, and I don't know what to do about it.'

66

What do you do about the men – always older men – who touch you? It's an amiable, almost paternal gesture in its way: a friendly arm around your shoulder or your waist, a pat on the head, some vague rearrangement of your hair . . .

The fatherly attitude behind these hugs is far more pernicious than the physical gestures themselves . . . All women, irrespective of age, are seen as dear creatures, nay daughters, who need bolstering, protection and encouragement . . .

> *'The attitude makes us unthreatening. It makes it easy for*
> *them to forget that we have good degrees, good ideas, that we are*
> *articulate, efficient and can be tough. Worst of all, it makes us*
> *women forget those things, however briefly.*

99

'First Person', *The Guardian, 2 October 1991*

A MORI survey for the GMB general union revealed that sixty-three per cent of women and sixty-two per cent of men think that 'touching a woman colleague while explaining things to her' was a very or fairly serious example of sexual harassment.

PIN-UPS

Pin-ups and swearing are two areas where men and women often do not see eye-to-eye. Women may find both objectionable, while men may not.

Jo Morris of the Trades Union Congress says:

66

> *Sometimes men refuse to accommodate their work surroundings*
> *to the arrival of a woman. Say it's been an all-male area, and*
> *there are lots of pin-ups and pornographic magazines lying*
> *around, and the language is rough. They may refuse to change –*
> *instead, they see it as 'the woman has to adapt'.*
>
> *My view is that what people do in their own time is their own*
> *business. But employers should say that pornographic magazines*
> *and pin-ups are not appropriate for workplaces.*

99

When Labour MP Clare Short first presented her 'page three bill', which would have banned newspapers from carrying pictures of 'naked or partially naked women in sexually provocative poses', she told the House of Commons about the experience of some young women: 'Every day they were subjected to men reading such newspapers in the office, and to them tittering and laughing and making rude remarks such as, "Show us your page threes then". Such women feel strongly that this Bill should be enacted.' Conservative MPs laughed.[25]

'I suggest that, of all the measures that have been proposed to the House during this Session, this Bill deserves the booby prize.' Conservative MP Robert Adley opposing Clare Short's 'page three bill'[26]

Even so, attitudes and practices are changing. It seems strange, for example, to recall that as recently as 1979 the *Yorkshire Miner* carried every month a large picture of a semi-naked woman, usually the relative of a pit worker.

British Rail chairman Sir Bob Reid has set an example in this field, making a point of personally taking down pin-ups when he sees them.

66

The sticking point for some of the senior male managers was the question of removal of objectionable pictures, posters and written material. There are very few women who have not faced the situation and so, well understand the need for such action. There are very few men who have ever been in the position of even going into an environment where there are pictures of naked or semi-naked men, let alone having to work in such surroundings.

99

Sir Bob Reid, Chairman of the Board of British Rail Directors[27]

'I am a shop steward and I work in a large factory. Until recently we had to put up with pictures of naked or half-naked women pasted up all over the place. After the women got together and made one hell of a fuss the *male* supervisor had them all taken down. The funny thing is that when one of my women friends got a picture of a naked man and pinned it over her locker, the men didn't like it. They said it was vulgar and pornographic.'

Letter to Clare Short, MP[28]

MORI's survey for the GMB general union revealed that forty-two per cent of women and thirty-seven per cent of men think that pinning up girlie calendars is a very or fairly serious example of sexual harassment.

OFFICE LOVE AFFAIRS

One area which can cause problems is when there is a love affair between a woman and a married superior. Technically this is *not* sexual harassment because the woman agrees, and indeed may be very willing.

But arguably a married boss who embarks on an affair with a more junior woman is abusing his power. And the woman can end up beached, with her career as well as her love-life ruined, if in the end he does not leave his wife.

The story of Sara Keays, once secretary to the top Conservative politician Cecil Parkinson, is a dramatic example. Parkinson asked Sara Keays to marry him, but then stayed with his wife. When Sara Keays became pregnant, he begged her to have an abortion. She ended up as a single parent, forced to abandon her ambition to become a Conservative MP herself.

66

Is it not interesting that you never hear of unmarried fathers, only unmarried mothers; or of men having illegitimate children, only women; that you do not hear of "fallen men", only "fallen women"?

99

Sara Keays[29]

Of course some men – including prominent politicians – do leave their wives for their secretaries. But at the outset of an office affair, who can tell what will happen?

'I had had the misfortune to fall in love with a married man and to believe his declarations of love and his solemn promises . . . My reputation was about to be thrown to the wolves and all Cecil and his colleagues cared about was that he should remain in office and protect himself.' Sara Keays[30]

'It is a very eccentric morality that a husband's promise to his mistress should take priority over his responsibilities to his wife and children . . .' *Daily Telegraph, 10 October 1983*[31]

LECTURERS AND THERAPISTS

Other tricky relationships which can involve abuses of power include love affairs between lecturers and students, and between doctors or therapists and their patients. Such affairs start with an imbalance in power and dependency, and often leave the weaker person – the student or patient – damaged.

A woman social worker told researchers what happened on a training course: 'Within weeks of the course starting, X [a teacher] had commenced an affair with one of the students in the group. She was highly flattered by his attention and made no secret of the relationship.

'The relationship continued until the end of the year, when he selected a new student from the incoming year.

'The student in our group felt both humiliated and bitter. She never really had much to do with the rest of us after that, and became a very irregular attender.'[32]

COUNTRIES TAKING A STAND

Many countries and organisations have now taken a stand against sexual harassment at work. Countries where sexual harassment is recognised as illegal include Britain and Northern Ireland, Australia, Belgium, Canada, France, Ireland, New Zealand and the USA.

In France, sexual harassment is a criminal offence, and a guilty person can be imprisoned for a year and fined 100,000 francs (about £11,000). But the French law defines sexual harassment very narrowly, as 'pressure exerted by an employer or a more senior person, to obtain sexual favours from an employee, for his benefit or for the benefit of a third person'.

In Belgium, employers are obliged by law to adopt measures to protect workers against sexual harassment. They must notify these measures to the workers' committee, or, if there is none, they must display them on noticeboards.

The measures should include:

* A declaration that sexual harassment in the workplace will not be tolerated

* The name of the person or department responsible for giving advice and support to victims in confidence

* The penalties which may be imposed on people guilty of sexual harassment.

THE EUROPEAN CODE

In 1991 the European Parliament approved a code of practice on how to combat sexual harassment. This code is aimed primarily at employers, since they are responsible for ensuring the dignity of men and women at work.

The code recommends that, after consulting trade unions or employees' representatives, employers should adopt policy statements against sexual harassment, and should develop procedures for dealing properly with complaints, including providing confidential counsellors to help people who are being harassed.

This code of practice will be a source of great clarity, comfort and confidence-building to victims now experiencing harassment. It marks a real step forward for working women in the 1990s in Europe. The labour market of the 1990s, the changes that are going on within it and the present skills shortage will mean that more women will be present at the workplace than ever before in the years to come. While that may mean more incidents of harassment it should also mean that women will have more influence to demand a strengthening of the national laws to combat harassment.

Christine Crawley, MEP,
addressing the European Parliament, 21 October 1991

SEXUAL HARASSMENT IN THE UK

The British government's position is set out in a booklet issued by the Department of Employment in 1992, titled *Sexual Harassment in the Workplace: A guide for employers*. It was drawn up in consultation with the Confederation of British Industry, the

Trades Union Congress and the Equal Opportunities Commission.

The guide urges employers to draw up a policy and procedures to combat sexual harassment. It is accompanied by a leaflet aimed at employees telling them what they can do if they are being harassed.

The guide was mailed to all companies with more than ten staff – some 100,000 companies. The omission of smaller companies was unfortunate: it is in these companies that women are often most vulnerable, especially if they are being harassed by the owner, as they have no one in management to turn to and are often non-unionised.

Employment minister Robert Jackson, who launched the guide, somewhat marred the occasion by saying at the press conference that wolf whistles and pin-ups might be acceptable in a 'totally all-male environment where no woman will stray'. The Equal Opportunities Commission commented, 'We can't think of any circumstances where it would be acceptable.'[33]

THE LAW

In Britain and Northern Ireland, there is no special law against sexual harassment, but there are various laws which people can use to obtain redress.

Many people have now taken cases, and the courts have repeatedly made decisions which recognise that sexual harassment is a prohibited activity.

There is information on how to go about using the law in Chapter Four.

Taking legal action can be a long and gruelling process. So most people – from women who are suffering sexual harassment to legal and other experts – regard the law as the last resort.

But court decisions against sexual harassment have had great advantages for women in general. First, they make a public statement that society finds sexual harassment unacceptable. Second, they act as a threat to stop individual harassers and to persuade companies they should deal with it effectively.

Pat, a radio producer, has had two serious experiences of sexual harassment, both from much older men. She says:

> *I'll tell you what really works best, from my experience. The first time I was sexually harassed, it went on for years and I just didn't know what to do. The second time, I turned to the man and I said, with a smile on my face, "I will have you for sexual harassment." He nearly died, and that stopped him in his tracks.*
>
> *I am very grateful to the women who fought the lonely path through the courts. Because they have made it possible for people like me to say that to him, and force him to stop. Because he was scared enough to know that this has been done and cases have been won, and it's been very, very embarrassing for people.*

TWO

Why do they do it?

Women are not to blame for sexual harassment.

Women often wrongly imagine that they must be bringing it on themselves: 'It must be something I am doing. But what?'

This unjustified feeling is often encouraged by the harasser and by others in the workplace.

When Susan was twenty-three, her boss started harassing her. 'He seemed incredibly old to me – my father's age. He was married with children, and physically very unattractive – double yuk! I loved the work, but he made my life a misery. He was constantly trying to grope me and I was trying to evade him. He'd do it in front of people, too. And I thought at the time that it was me, because nobody else seemed to think that this was at all unusual behaviour. It was all, "Don't worry about it, dear." It was only years later that I realised I could have got him the sack.'

Tania, a nineteen-year-old clerk who was harassed by her boss, said: 'The problem with sexual harassment is that it makes you doubt yourself. I kept thinking that it must have been my fault – I must have said the wrong thing, dressed the wrong way, I must have led him on.'

Tania was awarded £8,000 by an industrial tribunal.

A SOCIAL PROBLEM

The blame for sexual harassment lies with male power in society and with male views about women, as well as with the attitudes of organisations and of individuals.

Psychiatrist Dr Gillian Mezey says: 'Sexual harassment is a problem which mostly affects women. Men can experience it, but it's much rarer. One reason for that is because it appears to arise in situations where there is quite a significant difference in status and power between individual people within a workplace.

'Sexual harassment is a behaviour related to power, and power inequality. And you much more rarely find women who have that kind of authority and status over male colleagues.'

Some men harass over and over again. Some situations provoke harassment over and over again. And many organisations encourage harassment by tolerating it.

While this book was being researched, two women came forward separately who, it turned out, had both been harassed by the same man (a television producer). He had 'groped' one in 1970, and the other twenty years later. He is still working for the same company.

Sandra, his first victim, said: 'I didn't do anything about him, and I feel guilty about that now, because he did it again to his secretary and to other people. Everybody knew what he was like. But I was young and I was absolutely desperate to get on, and the last thing I wanted to do was rock the boat.'

So the way to end sexual harassment in the long term must be to make women and men equally powerful and to change the attitudes of individuals and organisations.

'I think that as long as women and black people are in lower grades, or not in the film and television industry at all, there will be problems. There must be a radical change inside the power structure of companies.' A reply to a questionnaire on sexual harassment by a media union

UNDERLYING PROBLEMS

There are various underlying problems, including these:

* Men (usually white heterosexuals) have political and economic power in society

* Men are conditioned to see women as sex objects and designed to serve their every need

* Men often see work as what *they* do, and the workplace as *their* province

* Sexual harassment is a form of bullying, and bullies pick on those they think are weak.

MALE POWER

Women go out of the home (where they are often less than equal) and into the workplace expecting to be treated as workers and colleagues, not sex objects or substitute wives. Nor do we expect to be constantly reminded that we are female.

Daisy, who left her job as an administrator in a charity after being constantly bullied by the director, remembers: 'He was always having affairs that went wrong, and he would come in and say things like, "You women all lie all the time," which I found outrageous. His attitude to any woman who came near the place was, was she good-looking? He used to say things like, "She's not good-looking enough to work in here." It was half a joke, but it half wasn't. And the very fact that he was saying it, I found a pressure.'

An activist in the women's liberation movement of the 1970s described her relationship to her boss:
'Men find me threatening. I mean, usually you're in a slightly inferior position to a man. His ego is constantly threatened, is constantly in a very dodgy state. And any sign of competence on my part is totally undermining of him. What I have to do is not appear to be competent. To make it appear that he's making the decisions and that he's having the ideas, and to be supportive, to sort of boost him along so that he can do things.'[34]

MEN IN THE ECONOMY

Women go into the workplace and find that after all they are not equal because men, generally speaking, have power there. Men are the bosses and the managers, who hire and fire. Lower down the hierarchy, they still usually have higher status and better pay than women.

* Ninety-nine per cent of managing directors of large companies are male

* Ninety-nine per cent of chief executives in local authorities are male

* Ninety-seven per cent of trade union general secretaries are male[35]

* Women form forty-three per cent of the labour force

* Their wages on average are one third less than men's.

JOB SEGREGATION

The British workforce is highly segregated along gender lines. Men dominate higher grades and their jobs are more highly paid than women's. Men are:

* Eighty per cent of scientists and engineers

* Ninety-five per cent of transport employees

* Ninety-nine per cent of construction and mining workers.

Women are segregated into lower grades and jobs which are paid less well than men's. Women are:

* Eighty-one per cent of caterers, cleaners and hairdressers

* Seventy-seven per cent of clerical workers

* Sixty-seven per cent of professionals in education, health and welfare

* Sixty-one per cent of sales staff.

A survey by the GMB general union discovered that in the food and drinks industry:

✱ Men predominate in the top grades in more than two-thirds of workplaces

✱ Women predominate in the top grades in only one in twenty workplaces

✱ Women predominate in the lowest grades in most factories.

Getting on in a job is more important than having children for nearly eighty per cent of women under thirty-five, according to a survey done for the National Council of Women of Great Britain. But the survey, which covered over a thousand women aged sixteen to seventy, also revealed that many women feel under-appreciated and under-used at work. Half said managers were not interested in their careers, and a third of those aged thirty-five to forty-four believed they had skills not being used.[36]

MEN IN POWER

Men's power in the workplace is reinforced by their power in society at large.

Men make the laws

In the House of Commons in 1993 there were 591 male MPs and sixty female MPs. There is a rifle range but no creche.

❝

If the Good Lord had intended us all having equal rights to go out to work and to behave equally, you know he really wouldn't have created man and woman.

❞

Patrick Jenkin, Conservative MP, during the 1979 election campaign, just before he became Secretary of State for Social Services

Men interpret and enforce the laws at the highest level

✱ All judges in the House of Lords are men, as are ninety-six per cent of judges in general

✷ Many lay magistrates are women.

Men dominate the media, which disseminate ideas about what women are like. In the broadcasting, film and video industry, men are:

✷ eighty-nine per cent of senior management in the BBC

✷ seventy-five per cent or more of producers and directors

✷ more than ninety-five per cent of camera staff.

66

A small number of white men control our media. They set the agenda, deciding what is or is not newsworthy. Women usually appear on the sidelines, as appendages to men; their role in news stories is undervalued . . . Issues which are of specific interest to women are seen as unimportant. Feminism and women's political initiatives are often treated dismissively or even abusively . . .

99

The Campaign for Press and Broadcasting Freedom
London Women's Group[37]

HISTORY

The problem of sexual harassment is not new. However early forms of society, when people lived in mobile and often-changing groups of 'hunter-gatherers', were probably free of it. Even though the sexes had different roles – the women gathering roots and berries, and looking after the children, while the men hunted – everyone had equal access to sources of food and no one was able to coerce anyone else.

The Hadza are a people in Tanzania. Dr James Woodburn described their lifestyle in around 1960, when many were still hunter-gatherers, moving often in a territory rich in food-sources:

'A husband goes away on a visit to some other part of the country without his wife at his peril. He may well find when he returns she has either married someone else or that she has repudiated him by putting on the dress of an unmarried girl to indicate her availability for marriage.'[38]

But with the development of agriculture and herding, things changed. As people became tied down by land or property or both, men often appropriated control of it, and also of women.

SLAVERY

The more power men – or a particular group of men – had in society, the more power they had over women.

Under plantation slavery in the eighteenth and nineteenth century in the USA and the Caribbean, white male slave-owners and overseers exploited women slaves not only as workers but also for sex.

Slave women resisted the advances of white men. But they risked cruel punishment.

One Jamaican girl was put in the stocks when she refused to comply with the sexual demands of a small plantation owner – who in fact was her half-brother. She continued to resist his entreaties, and was unmercifully flogged. Afterwards she complained to the magistrate, but the man went unpunished.[39]

White men regarded interracial sex as their prerogative, and took it by force. But if white women and slave men tried it, even consenting, the penalties were extreme.

The planter John Stedman commented that 'should it be known that any European female had an intercourse with a slave of any denomination', she is 'forever detested and the slave loses his life without mercy'.[40]

PREDATORY IMPERIALISTS

As nineteenth century European imperialists colonised the globe, they preyed on the women – and often the boys – of the peoples they were trying to subdue, provoking revolts, strikes and suicides.

In Afghanistan in September 1842, British soldiers took revenge for a humiliating defeat earlier in the year by destroying

Kabul, indiscriminately killing many people, and raping many women.[41]

On tea and sugar plantations, many planters sexually exploited women labourers. In 1914 Tamils went on strike in Malaya, demanding, among other things, an end to such molestation.

Suicide was a common form of protest on plantations against this and other abuses of the system.[42]

VICTORIAN MORALITY

Back in the metropolis, the Victorian paterfamilias had a similar attitude to the slave owners and planters, regarding the servant girl as easy pickings.

Most were young single women and many were orphans. Their work was low status and low paid. Their vulnerability was increased by the fact that they usually 'lived in', were not unionised and had little legal protection.

Their only real power, when mistreated sexually or otherwise, was their ability to change jobs – which they did frequently.[43]

In the Lancashire cotton mills, women took more abrasive action. In January 1887, sixty-eight women and men from the Henshaw Street Spinning Company walked out, demanding an investigation into the behaviour of a male carder, Robert Yates, who had sexually pressured and indecently assaulted twelve young women under his authority.

The company sacked the strikers and hired scabs to replace them.

Yates ended up in court, and one woman testified: 'On the 18th December he got me in the store room, and asked me to sew a button on his trousers. (Laughter.) He asked me to go in, and I went in, and whilst I was threading the needle he began to use dirty language, and also behaved indecently.'

The court also heard that Yates 'knew that it was absolutely impossible for him to be caught and stopped in his actions if he pursued a similar method from then till doomsday . . . his method in all cases being to make improper overtures, and on refusal to pick a quarrel, which is always easy, and then to either discharge them at once or with a week's notice.'

Yates's defence counsel called the women sexually precocious, and insisted they were willing partners. Yates, he insisted, was merely 'marlocking' – flirting or being playful.

Yates was fined £5 plus court costs, and got the sack. But the workers who had gone on strike were not rehired.[44]

THE GROPING BOSS

Today, as in Victorian days, some men take advantage of their position to demand sexual favours. When they are rejected, they can get nasty.

'You often get complaints about sexual harassment that are originated by suggestive remarks or invitations to go out to dinner or to bed, which have been refused, and it then turns into a complaint about him being quite unreasonable about the standards of her work, or time-keeping, or whatever.' Jo Morris, TUC

The sixty-year-old manager of a printshop started harassing Harriet, a sixteen-year-old sales assistant, as soon as she started her job. He harassed several of her colleagues too. Harriet said: 'He would even put his hand inside your blouse, on your shoulder, put his arm round you. When I finally started to pull away and make it clear I didn't want it, he started to get nasty. Then he gave me the bad jobs, and it culminated in him shouting at me and threatening to sack me in front of some customers.'

Harriet left her job and went to a law centre. When he heard she was taking legal action, the manager offered her £750, which she accepted.

The 'casting couch' routine is by no means restricted to the theatre.

'When I was a student, I applied for a scholarship to do postgraduate work in a Latin-American country. I had lunch with the ambassador of that country – he was about sixty years old – and he put his hand on my leg and invited me to go on holiday with him. I didn't go on holiday, and I didn't get the scholarship.' Maxine, journalist

MALE SENIORITY

If men – as all too often happens – are senior, women have to take their superior power into account when dealing with them. To say no – or, even worse, to complain – may be to risk dismissal or jeopardise one's chances of promotion.

This is why women need support – from colleagues, from trade unions, from management, and from the law.

Heather was working as a secretary in an engineering firm when her husband developed cancer and died. She was harassed by her boss before and after her husband's death, but stayed in the job because she had two daughters to support.

She went to an industrial tribunal and told them: 'He would ask me, "How about a blow job?", or "How about a legover?" On one occasion he said, "I've a lump in my trousers, do something about it." He offered to "help me out" if I was sexually frustrated. He stroked my leg on several occasions. I tried to be tactful, but to make it clear that I was not interested. If I protested, it only seemed to encourage him.'

The tribunal heard that after her husband died, her boss grabbed her breasts on three occasions, and she shouted at him to stop. When she asked for a pay rise, 'he replied, "Drop your drawers and the pay rise is yours."' Eventually he sacked her.

The tribunal ruled against Heather because she had no witness to the assaults and because she stayed in the job. She plans to appeal.

As a young television presenter, Pat had a serious problem with a producer. 'He was in his late sixties, and seemed a very nice old man. Then he started to give me a big grandpa-like hug in the office, which made me very uncomfortable. Then he would say "I am so fond of you, you're just like the daughter I never had," and he would start to get breathless. It was not nice at all.

'But I thought, "If I pull rank and get shirty and shitty, I might not be taken on for the next series." I was dependent on him. I was forever stepping round the table to avoid him. Once he even grabbed me in the hospitality room. I got really resentful.'

ECONOMIC CLIMATE

Being 'shirty or shitty' is a particular problem in times of recession, when jobs are scarce and unions are weakened.

Daisy walked out of her job as a charity administrator in 1992 after being bullied. She says: 'I'm really glad I left, and I wish I had done it before. But at the moment, it's not easy to walk out, because there are so few jobs. Luckily I found a new job fairly quickly, and I'm really enjoying it. It's quite a shock to work with nice people!'

In times of high employment, or if you personally are much in demand, it's much easier to tell the harasser to 'get stuffed' – or words to that effect.

> **66**
>
> *When I went recently to present myself to the producer of a well-known TV series at his request, or so I supposed, he sneaked in a wet kiss and a clutch at my breasts as an exercise of his power, a privilege which he could not have exacted from any of the men who have appeared on the same programme. I have since instructed my agent to turn down any offer of work from him, but most girls would not be in a position to do that.*
>
> **99**
>
> Germaine Greer, writing in 1970[45]

PICKING ON THE WEAK

The 'groping boss' will usually inflict his unwanted attentions on a woman who is in a weaker position than him, in part because she is less likely to hit back.

'They pick on people like me because it's so much easier. It's not so much hassle, because there won't be so much come-back. Because it's generally people like me who won't report it, because you want to get on and you want to keep your job. And you are low down the ladder. It's just the way it happens.' Sandra, television company employee

Queen's University researchers analysed twenty-eight cases refer-red to the Equal Opportunities Commission for Northern Ireland. The complainants were mostly young, and included three men. Some had been harassed by more than one man.

The researchers concluded that while it was difficult to generalise about the victims, the characteristics of the harassers were much more predictable. They were all men, typically over thirty, and 'normally in positions of authority over the person who was harassed'.[46]

DELIBERATE MANOEUVRES

There are many stories of men deliberately manoeuvring women into being alone with them, and also trying to make them susceptible to their demands by hinting at career advancement.

The woman may not be aware of what he is up to. She may take him at face value, and then realise with a terrible shock that she has been misled.

Jane, a computer operator and member of the GMB general union, recalls:

66

Because my company was moving offices, I agreed to complete an important job at home with a male colleague. Unfortunately the guy had more than work on his mind. He turned up with two bottles of champagne. He kept saying he had a lot to offer and he could teach me a lot. He then produced some condoms and said he'd bought them that morning in case I wasn't covered. I told my union rep and she reported him. He's gone now.[47]

99

A NOD AND A WINK

The problem becomes acute when advancement depends on a good report or reference, or in industries like the media, where jobs are eagerly sought and often depend on a nod and a wink, and where contracts are short.

Christine remembers:

> *I was a presenter on a local TV programme. A senior editor invited me out for dinner, to discuss a new strand of programmes, or so he said. I was new and I didn't know his reputation, so I took him at his word.*
>
> *I met him in a pub, and there were a lot of other journalists there, who were obviously thinking, "Oh, she's the next one!". Then we went for dinner and I realised there was no suggestion of a new strand in his area, and that I had been completely duped.*
>
> *I felt so demeaned, that other journalists should have thought I was having a relationship with him. And I couldn't even say to him, "What the hell do you think you're doing?", because of his position of authority in the organisation.*
>
> *The whole experience was awful.'*

GROUP HARASSMENT

Harassment of women by groups of men is common where women are moving into previously all-male workplaces, such as the printing industry, construction, the post office, the railways, the fire brigade or the police force. Instinctively, it seems, men often respond by trying to exclude women from 'their' territory.

There are some horrendous stories of persecution.

In 1985 Karen became one of only two women train drivers with British Rail. There was also one woman relief driver and about six women driver's assistants.

A male colleague sexually assaulted her when she was driving a train at fifty mph. He was sacked, but because she had reported him, her colleagues shunned her and made vile jokes. One pushed a pornographic magazine close up to her face when she was in the mess room eating her sandwiches.

Lynne, aged twenty-two, was one of the first three women to become firefighters in London. She was subjected to a horrific ordeal by male firefighters, which included pouring a bucket of urine over her and masturbating in front of her. She complained and was transferred to another station, where she was ostracised and further abused. She went off sick with depression.

Lynne took the Greater London Council and the firemen in question to court, claiming assault, battery and false imprisonment. They settled out of court, with the GLC paying her £25,000 and the firemen paying her £2,100 between them.

An ambulance woman replied to a survey by her union that 'ninety-five per cent of the lads are great, but a handful find it difficult to just let us get on with our job'.

Women are coming into male-dominated industries in some cases as a result of equal opportunities policies. In other cases, employers find it cheaper to employ women. A prime example is the printing industry, where young women have keyboarding skills which are suited to new printing technologies: employers find it cheaper to bring them in than to train the men to type.

In one case of long-running harassment in the printing industry, male workers put a paper flag on a young woman's desk – to indicate that she had her period.

In another case, a young woman with strong religious convictions wore her boyfriend's jacket to work, and male workers put condoms in the pocket, which her boyfriend found.

In yet another case, a young woman printer used to find pornographic pictures pinned to her machine.

MORI's survey for the GMB general union revealed that thirty-two per cent of women, but only sixteen per cent of men, think that a common cause of sexual harassment is 'men resenting women for taking "men's jobs"'.

LAW MAKERS – LAW BREAKERS?

Group harassment occurs in many parts of society.

Jane, a forty-seven-year-old police constable, resigned from the force in 1989 claiming she had been hounded out by a campaign of abuse by male officers in Bedfordshire. Their prejudice, sexist remarks and insults had hampered her career and made her life a misery, she said.

Sergeant Alan Wheatman was dismissed from the Metropolitan Police in 1992 after charges were brought following allegations that he had made sexist and abusive remarks to women officers at Chelsea police station between 1988 and 1990.

In the House of Commons, too, men see women as invading a male club.

When Clare Short MP presented her bill to ban 'page three' pictures from papers, male MPs shouted comments about her figure. Teresa Gorman MP has said of the sexist heckling: 'It's schoolboy stuff but there's a nasty edge to it. With male MPs they attack what they say; with women MPs they attack what they look like. It can be savage.'[48]

If the people who make the laws harass women, what hope is there for the rest of us?

Because of the risk of harassment, trade unionists and others concerned with workers' lives emphasise that women going into previously all-male workplaces must have management support, and their male co-workers must be given training to help them adjust to working alongside women.

The same applies when black people are going into previously all-white workplaces, or disabled people are going into a workplace where everyone is able-bodied.

MANAGEMENT'S LIABILITY

Harassment does not occur in a vacuum. Major problems are that colleagues often collude and management turns a blind eye.

66

A few years ago I made an official complaint to my boss about a particular member of staff. The advice? I was told it really wouldn't be advisable to continue with the complaint; this member of staff had had lots of complaints against him – but allowances had to be made, and I wouldn't want to rock the boat in my position, would I?!

99

Meryl, freelance worker

Psychiatrist Dr Gillian Mezey says: *You find organisations which you could call harassment-prone, where there's a collusive atmosphere. It's not that people are being told, "It's all right to harass", but there is a feeling that this sort of behaviour is not going to be punished, and that the men who harass are simply doing something which perhaps other men might do in a similar situation.*

'And when these women complain, there is often a kind of scape-goating of the victim. People group together around the perpetrator, to protect him.

'They may blame the woman – call her the "office tart" and that sort of thing. And then the organisation will often get rid of the victim and say, "We're getting rid of the problem." Whereas of course the problem is in the harasser, and he will just continue to do the same to other women.'

'We have found that certain doctors harass the nurses, and it has a snowball effect, in that otherwise normal members of staff join in.' A reply to a survey by a health service union

SIDING WITH THE HARASSER

Management will tend to side with the man (or men) who harasses. Firstly, because management – usually also being male – will instinctively side with them. Secondly, it may seem less disruptive – and cheaper – to side with the senior person or the group that is in a majority. So the woman may well find herself moved to another job, while the man stays in place.

'We have a consultant who is generally free with his hands. If he were a porter, he would have been sacked – but as a consultant, he gets away with it.' A reply to a survey by a health service union

Researchers at the Manchester School of Management surveyed 110 top companies. They found that:

* The most common punishment for someone found guilty of harassment was either an official or unofficial warning

* The next most likely outcome was no action whatsoever, as forty-nine per cent maintained that there was some likelihood that nothing would be done

* More than half (fifty-four per cent) said that the harasser never faced dismissal

* The victim of sexual harassment was more likely to be moved than the harasser.

A shop assistant sold forty pairs of socks in three days to a lecherous man, and became so concerned that she told her managers. They laughed off her fears, but on the fourth day the man attacked her as she was going home.

LEGAL OBLIGATION

But it can be illegal for an employer not to take action.

Mrs Darby had worked for thirteen years for a small company called Bracebridge Engineering, when she was sexually assaulted by two male supervisors, Mr Daly and Mr Smith.

The two men grabbed her and carried her to an office, where they blocked the door. Mr Daly put his hand between her legs and touched her private parts, remarking, 'You've got a big one.' Eventually she managed to escape.

Mrs Darby complained to the general manager, Miss Reynolds, who did nothing, because the men denied the incident. Mrs Darby resigned and went to a tribunal, which upheld her complaints, as did an appeal tribunal. She was awarded £3,900 for unfair dismissal and £150 for sex discrimination.

The appeal tribunal said that her employer's failure to act was a breach of contract, since there is a mutual obligation in every employment contract of trust, confidence and support, and the employer had an obligation not to undermine the confidence of female staff.

A survey by a health service union found that of those who reported sexual harassment to management or the union:

* Half said it made the situation better

* A third said it made no change

* The rest (less than a fifth) said it made the situation worse.

MALE ATTITUDES

Why do men harass? Why do colleagues and organisations collude? Part of the answer must lie in male attitudes to women.

Psychiatrist Dr Gillian Mezey says:

> *Many of the views held by harassers, particularly in relation to women – women's roles, attitudes about women's independence, ideas about femininity – are very traditional, very conservative. And also they hold myths about rape and sexual violence towards women, such as "women enjoy it", that are also held by rapists.*

STEREOTYPES

The conservative British view of men and women sees them as opposites. Men are supposed to be superior, women inferior; men strong, women weak; men intellectual, women instinctive; men active, women passive; men unemotional, women emotional; men at work, women in the home . . . and so on.

These stereotypes are in part a product of the nineteenth century, a time when women's rights declined to almost zero while their menfolk set forth to colonise the globe.

Historian Ronald Hyam writes: 'Early Victorian men were fairly sentimental in their friendships. They walked about arm-in-arm (as much of the rest of the world outside the Anglo-Saxon nations still does); they described themselves in their letters as "loving friends" . . . They were not much given to competitive sport . . . They had no fear of tears.'[49]

The Victorians applied the same negative characteristics to black people and Irish people as they did to women. Indeed, Celts were often described as 'feminine' – hence needing to be ruled by 'masculine' Anglo-Saxons.

JUSTIFICATION

Describing women – or black or colonised people – as inferior is a way of saying it is acceptable to dominate and exploit them.

Men certainly benefit hugely from women's labour, both in the workplace and the home.

Men are half the world's population but:

* hold ninety-nine per cent of the world's property

* receive ninety per cent of the world's incomes

* do a third of the world's work hours.[50]

In her famous book *The Second Sex*, published in 1949, French philosopher Simone de Beauvoir wrote:

> *there are deep similarities between the situation of woman and that of the Negro. Both are being emancipated today from a like paternalism, and the former master class wishes to "keep them in their place" – that is, the place chosen for them. In both cases the former masters lavish more or less sincere eulogies, either on the virtues of "the good Negro" with his dormant, childish, merry soul – the submissive Negro – or on the merits of the woman who is "truly feminine" – that is, frivolous, infantile, irresponsible – the submissive woman. In both cases the dominant class bases its argument on a state of affairs that it has itself created . . . Yes, women on the whole **are** today inferior to men; that is, their situation affords them fewer possibilities. The question is: should that state of affairs continue?[51]*

MALE-BONDING

Today male-bonding – the formation of male friendships – often depends on seeing women as different or 'other'. 'Birds' are out there to be consumed, along with cars, drink and football. Or they are 'nagging wives' or mothers-in-law, to be escaped from.

In particularly 'macho' occupations, such as the army, the view of women is often especially crude.

Former paratrooper Michael Asher describes how his fellow soldiers used to hold 'grot contests':

> **"**
>
> *The lads would meet together in an Aldershot pub and have a few drinks, then scatter round the town searching for women. The object was to see who could pick up the most nauseatingly ugly girl. No one was immune from the Paras' humour. They would bring their escorts back to a certain pub at a certain time, and over the next round of drinks would judge the "grot" of the evening. The crowning act of utter obscenity was to obtain a woman's hand-bag under some pretext and defecate into it.*[52]
>
> **"**

MALE PRIDE

Men in all-male workplaces often develop a distinctive culture, which excludes women. The arrival of a woman gives them a choice: either they can alter their behaviour, or they can 'gang up' against her. All too often they choose the latter.

Researchers noted that among male workers in a Tyneside shipyard, certain topics of conversation – current affairs, sport and sex – constantly recurred. Persistent awkwardness or ignorance incurred a social penalty. There was often horseplay – mock fighting, mock kissing, mock embracing.[53]

For men in traditionally all-male occupations – whether soldiers, policemen, firefighters, engine-drivers, construction workers or printers – their very pride in themselves may be linked to the fact that they are doing jobs which 'women can't do'.

The arrival of women doing the same job not only breaks up

the all-male group, but may also be a blow to men's sense of identity and self-esteem. Rather than adapt to the idea that men and women are equal, men may respond to these situations by tormenting women in an offensively sexist way, to put them down or drive them out. 'Normal' blokes turn into monsters overnight.

Tracey, a young bricklayer with a south London council, was subjected to constant harassment. Comments included, 'You've got a nice arse', 'What are you anyway? A dyke?', and even, 'Does your spirit-level fit up your cunt?'

They started to make thrusting movements with their hips when she entered the shed. She put up with the harassment for a long time, but eventually became a nervous wreck. She went to a tribunal and was awarded £15,000 in an out-of-court settlement.

In 'group bullying' situations, men persecute women who are doing the same work as themselves, rather than women who are doing 'typically female' work, such as cleaning or secretarial work.

A Home Office report concluded: 'Nearly all police women experienced some form of sexual harassment from police men and this was at a significantly greater rate than that to which other women working within the police were exposed.'[54]

In such contexts, sexual harassment becomes a kind of psychological warfare designed to 'put women back in their place'.

66

One of the benefits that oppression confers upon the oppressors is that the most humble among them is made to feel *superior; thus, a "poor white" in the* [American] *South can console himself with the thought that he is not a "dirty nigger" . . . Similarly, the most mediocre of males feels himself a demigod as compared with women.*

99

Simone de Beauvoir, *The Second Sex*[55]

But men who harass women when they are part of an all-male group often behave quite reasonably in other situations.

Rosemary, twenty-two years old, was harassed by three young men who worked in the same printing firm. They called her names like 'Fathead', 'Thicko', 'Shit for Brains' and 'Bimbo', and retched loudly when she passed them. She became very depressed and went off sick.

Yet outside work, as she told an industrial tribunal, their behaviour was not objectionable. One of the men could be quite friendly towards her. But in work, in the company of the other two, he behaved quite differently.

Rosemary won her tribunal case, assisted by the print union, the GPMU, and by the Equal Opportunities Commission for Northern Ireland.

MEDIA STEREOTYPES

The media – from 'page three' in the tabloids to the news on television – constantly reinforce the image of women as sex objects, and downgrade their brains and skills.

Classic examples are the purveyors of news and weather bulletins on television. The men are allowed to have grey hair, eccentric or plain faces and lumpy figures; but the women must be pretty, slim and well-groomed.

When TV newsreader Fiona Armstrong got an £150,000-a-year job as an early-morning presenter for GMTV, company executives remade her image. Director of programmes Lis Howell told the press, 'We encouraged Fiona to wear brighter colours and shorter skirts because she's got great legs.' And to make her smile more, Fiona Armstrong was told 'to chew on a coathanger'.

Lis Howell said, 'I want the viewers to fancy the presenters.'

Jill Parkin of the *Daily Express* wrote caustically that Howell 'says she's going for the F-factor, which is now hastily being reglossed as Fanciability, but was somewhat more Anglo-Saxon and asterisk-worthy when it was first used.'[56]

But as it happened, the TV station's ratings did not rise. Lis Howell resigned, and her successor rejected her 'F-factor' concept.[57] Later, Fiona Armstrong also resigned.

WHO'S ASKING FOR IT?

Men of the 'groping boss' variety will often defend themselves by saying 'she was asking for it'.

Psychological studies done in the USA suggest that men often imagine that women are giving them a sexual 'come-on' when in fact they are not. Furthermore, they continue to believe the woman is 'asking for it' even if she rejects their advances.[58]

John, a fifty-four-year-old assistant manager, said:

❝

I was moved from my old department after a woman accused me of sexually harassing her. I was only joking around. OK, maybe I was a little near the knuckle . . . I could see she was upset when I tried to kiss her . . . but I just thought she'd lost her sense of humour. No, I wouldn't do anything like it again. It's ruined my career and I've been labelled a 'dirty old man'.[59]

❞

A MORI survey for the GMB general union revealed that fifty per cent of men and fifty-four per cent of women think that a common cause of sexual harassment is 'men not understanding what women find offensive'.

Lawyers and trade unionists who specialise in developing policies and procedures on sexual harassment agree that it is *absolutely out of order*, when investigating complaints, to ask the complainant questions like:

❋ What were you wearing at the time?

❋ Did you do anything to lead him on?

❋ Surely he was only joking?[60]

There has been one problematic legal decision at the Employment Appeal Tribunal on the question of clothing.

Karen Wileman went to an industrial tribunal after she had been harassed for four years by one of the directors of Minilec Engineering. She told the tribunal Mr Attwell had made salacious remarks, rubbed up against her, fondled her hands, given her 'saucy' books, asked her to go out with him, and talked about pornographic videos.

The all-male tribunal agreed that she had been sexually harassed, but only awarded her £50 for injury to feelings on the grounds that the harassment had only been a minor irritation to her, and that she had occasionally worn 'scanty and provocative' clothing to work. Karen still denies this, and is angry about it.

The tribunal made their decision despite the fact that the harasser had told them he did not notice her clothes much. Nor did they allow Karen to call evidence of how he had allegedly harassed other women.

The Employment Appeal Tribunal upheld the decision.

SEXUAL URGES

There is a widespread but misguided belief that men are driven to grope by their 'sexual urges'.

'We have sexual urges too, and we don't go round putting our hands down men's trousers!' Anna, librarian

Author Naomi Wolf believes that the training of modern men and women has a lot to answer for:
'Men are visually aroused by women's bodies and less sensitive to their arousal by women's personalities because they are trained early into that response, while women are less visually aroused and more emotionally aroused because that is their training.'
She goes on to say: 'One trouble with soft-core sexual imagery aimed at young men is that the women photographed are not actually responding sexually to anything; young men grow up trained to eroticize images that teach them nothing about female desire.' Consequently, 'men are exaggeratedly insensitive to female desire' for their own arousal.[61]

Many gropers will grope almost anyone junior who hoves into view. Their targets do not need to be particularly 'sexy' or dress in a 'provocative' way. They just need to be women.
Jill Chesworth, a press officer at the Equal Opportunities Commission, remembers: 'We had a case in a very small branch

office. About six women worked there, and one man – who of course was the branch manager.

'One of the women was getting sexually harassed by him, and she came to us for advice. One of the first pieces of advice we give is, **"Talk to other people about it in the working environment, because it quite often happens to someone else."**

'She found out that all six women were being sexually harassed!'

DRASTIC MEASURES

But unfortunately women often do imagine they are in some way to blame for 'provoking' men, and sometimes go to extreme lengths to make themselves unattractive in order to avoid further harassment.

Tania, a nineteen-year-old office clerk, found herself working for a man who had spent twenty-five years in the army and kept cracking vulgar and sexual jokes. He began asking her to have sex, commenting on her 'boobs', and pushing against her. Both union and management were unhelpful, and she ended up going to a tribunal which awarded her £8,000.

But, she says: 'I haven't worked since it happened, and I lost four stone and became anorexic. I lost weight because I thought it would make me less attractive, and I didn't bother to do my hair. I still feel very unsure if I'm left alone with a man.'

Twenty years after she was seriously harassed, Susan is still affected by it. She says, 'I love clothes, but I tend not to wear anything that might be read wrong.'

After Sandra was harassed by a man who had been harassing young women for twenty years, she was told by a female manager to cover up her body in order not to attract his attention. She says: 'I basically stopped wearing skirts at work. I always wore my jeans, or a pair of leggings and a massive shirt which came down to my knees, and there was no way you could see the shape of any part of my body. It was so unfair. It was very hot and the blokes were going round in a pair of shorts and nothing else.'

But changing her appearance did not solve Sandra's problems. She found herself being bullied and was forced to leave her job.

SEXUAL HARASSMENT AND DRESS

Women often feel that they can't win. If we look good, we risk attracting unwelcome and intrusive advances. If we don't conform to the stereotype of the 'ideal woman', we may be insulted on that account.

Working as we do in a 'man's world', many women feel obliged to dress as men apparently want them to dress. Indeed, some employers – from television stations to bars and casinos – try to force women to dress in a 'sexy' way.

Helen and four other waitresses at a London wine bar were told to work in their bra and pants for a businessmen's party. Helen refused, and her boss fired her. She took legal action and won £6,300 for sex discrimination. Helen observed, 'You have to hold onto some self-respect.'

Mrs Robertson and Mrs Leaper were sacked from their jobs as bar staff because they refused to wear new uniforms that they thought were degrading. Their old uniform was a long tartan skirt, and the new uniform was supposed to be a peasant outfit. It included a striped orange blouse with an elasticated neckline. The two women took legal action, and a tribunal recorded Mrs Leaper's reaction to the blouse: it was 'like a balloon, hideous, of cheap material, and without style. She was mortified at the prospect of having to wear it.'

The tribunal decided that they did not have to wear *any* uniform provided by the employer, but came to the curious conclusion that they had contributed to their dismissal by twenty-five per cent!

FREEDOM OF DRESS

What we want is the freedom to dress as we wish, and to look attractive without being molested.

> 66
>
> *It's so frustrating. It's not that you want to go to work dressed like you're going for a night out. But why can't you look reasonably different or attractive or feminine even, when you're doing a job? It's just not right that we should have to constantly think about how men are going to react to us.*
>
> 99
>
> Sandra

Feminist psychotherapist Susie Orbach comments: 'In a world that designates women as the sexual object for both sexes, in a world obsessed by its fantasies of female sexuality, presenting oneself in sexually attractive ways is a route to garner some self-esteem.

'But that doesn't mean that women invite or wish for persistent, unwanted sexual innuendo, touching or attention of a sexual nature.

'By the same account, women who dare to turn their back on presenting themselves in a "sexual" manner do not invite the vicious intrusion implied in "what you need is a good fuck" comments.'[62]

'The striking asexuality of the female achiever's wardrobe is explained by this apparent inability of the British male to deal with female sexuality.' Lowri Turner, *London Evening Standard*[63]

'Clothing that highlights women's sexuality will be casual wear when women's sexuality is under our own control ... Women will thoughtlessly be able to adorn ourselves with pretty objects when there is no question that we are not objects.'[64] Naomi Wolf, *The Beauty Myth*

THREE

Sexual harassment: what can we do about it?

Obviously the long-term solution to sexual harassment is for women to have equality with men in society, and for a major change in attitudes. But as most of us can't wait for that happy day, immediate 'first aid' is needed.

There are in fact many things we can do, either on our own, or with the help of friends, colleagues, unions, management or an outside agency. As the last resort, we can take legal action.

What most of us want to do, when we are faced with harassment, is to put a stop to it as quickly as possible so as to create a pleasant working environment.

Usually, we want to stay in our jobs if at all possible, and to solve the problem with a minimum of fuss. We want our relationships with our colleagues to stay smooth, and we want to limit the damage to our self-confidence. In short, we just want to be able to get on with *living*!

How easily we can achieve this very much depends on the circumstances, and on whether we have the support of unions and management.

STANDARD ADVICE

The standard advice given by professionals dealing with sexual harassment applies whether you are dealing with one or more harassers. It includes:

✳ Make sure the harasser (or harassers) is informed – by you or someone else – that you dislike his behaviour. He must be told to stop.

✱ Tell him in writing (and keep a copy of the letter) if you find it easier.

✱ If you confront the harasser in person, you could take someone such as a union representative, or someone more senior in the office, with you.

✱ If there is a colleague you trust, you could confide in her or him. You may find other people are being harassed by the same man.

✱ Keep a note of the date and time of each incident of harassment, with details of what the harasser did and said.

✱ Tell your union representative, if you have one. If your rep is – or might be – unsympathetic, speak to someone higher up in the union, at regional or national level. Many unions have equality officers or women's officers. Some unions have special sexual harassment counsellors.

✱ Report the harasser to someone in authority in your organisation, or – if you are in a union – ask a union representative to do so. Even if the senior person takes no effective measures, this is an important step should you ever wish to take legal action.

✱ If you have no union and no-one to turn to in your company, or if your union or company is unhelpful, you can contact an outside advice agency, such as a Citizen's Advice Bureau, the Equal Opportunities Commission (or the Equal Opportunities Commission for Northern Ireland, if you live there), a law centre, or a women's organisation. (There is a list of useful organisations at the end of this book, see pages 81–85 and page 111.)

✱ If the harasser touches you on an intimate part of your body, you could report him to the police for indecent assault.

From the moment you take action of any kind, you need to bear in mind that, if it doesn't work, you may need to take matters further. The thought that there are several options may give you confidence in dealing with the harasser, and indeed your determination may help to persuade him to back off.

WITH THE HELP OF FRIENDS

From the time the harassment starts, it is a good idea to talk to people you trust – friends outside work, members of your family, or colleagues – about what is happening. They can give you support and make you feel you are not alone. And you will probably soon find other women who have had similar problems.

If you talk to colleagues, you may find that the man has harassed other women too. You may then be able to take joint action. And, if you end up taking legal action, another woman whom he has harassed may be willing to give evidence in your support.

Sharon, a single parent, got a job through a government scheme with a charity in the north-east of England. The chairman, a domineering older man, had the odd habit of inviting staff into the loo for one-to-one meetings.

He invited Sharon into the loo and offered to sign a form saying she was working more hours than she actually was, so that she could qualify for increased family credit. Two weeks later he offered her promotion. She said: 'Then he started groping me. He stuck his hands all over my breasts. I was very upset and bolted out of the loo.'

Next she was told her son could no longer have a free place in the charity's creche.

A woman colleague saw how upset she was and asked what had happened. Sharon told her – and the woman said he had done the same thing to her! The two went to see their senior – who said the chairman had done the same thing to her too!

All three then reported the matter to a member of the management committee. She told the chairman he had been accused of sexual harassment, and next day all three women were sacked!

They then threatened to report the case to the Director of Social Services, and the next day the chairman resigned.

THE FIRST STEP

Everyone involved professionally with sexual harassment advises that the first step we must take is make sure the harasser is told – perhaps in writing – that his behaviour is unacceptable.

We may do this ourselves, or we may get a union or management representative to, but one way or another he – or they, if there is more than one harasser – *must be told.*

For a start, he may simply not realise that his behaviour is unacceptable. And secondly, unless you take some kind of action, he is likely to carry on, and may well get worse.

A health service union asked members how they had responded to sexual harassment, and noted:

'Ignoring it, going along with it, or making a joke of it, generally made the situation worse or made no change to it. "I endured his comments for weeks, and did and said nothing. It gradually got worse. He began to touch me, grab me, etc. I was too scared to tell anyone – I was scared they wouldn't believe me."'

Sarah, a nineteen-year-old shop assistant in a supermarket in Scotland, was harassed by the forty-year-old manager.

She told a tribunal that he had asked her to come through the back 'for a poke', and constantly made remarks about the size of her chest, like 'they are bouncing well today' and 'you wouldn't drown anyway'. One day he had followed her into the chill room and shut the door, then rubbed his hand on the zip of his trousers, saying, 'Come on, Sarah'. On another occasion, when she asked a question about her pay, he said, 'Come on through the back, get on your back and open your legs, I'll see what I can do.'

Sarah decided to ignore him completely and thought if she did he would stop harassing her and leave her alone. However, this was not the case. In fact he got worse.

Backed by USDAW, Sarah went to an industrial tribunal and was awarded £3,794.

STRESS

The psychological effects of 'putting up with it' can be dire. As we saw earlier, it can undermine your self-confidence, put you under constant stress, and lead in some cases to severe disorders such as depression and anorexia.

Also, the longer you 'put up with it', and the more stressed you become, the less able you may feel to take action.

Dr Mezey says:

66

If the sexual harassment is undermining a woman's self-esteem and sense of effectiveness, then she's going to become progressively less able to put a stop to it. And she may begin to feel guilty, because she will see herself as colluding in the process. Unless she puts a stop to it very early, she will increasingly fear that she is going to be blamed if she does complain.

99

And you may end up sacked anyway, or feel forced to walk out.

TAKING ACTION YOURSELF

Saying something to the harasser, in writing or otherwise, can be very difficult, especially if the guy is your boss and if you are desperate to keep your job.

Psychiatrist Dr Gillian Mezey says: 'It's much easier to tell the harasser to stop if he's your equal or your junior. But if you fear that it is going to have very negative consequences for you – like you're not going to get promoted, or you're going to be moved into an area you don't want to be moved into, or you might even be fired – then it is clearly much more difficult.'

If you are dealing with a senior person and you are afraid of the effects of confronting him, it may be a good idea to try to find someone experienced to help you, either through your union or an outside agency.

HITTING OUT

'Bottling it up' can also lead to women releasing their pent-up emotions by violently attacking the harasser. This gives them the satisfaction of 'getting their own back' but is likely also to terminate their employment!

Susan, in her early twenties, was harassed by her much older boss for about three years. She says:

66

It started off innocently enough – he would put his arm round my shoulder. I just ignored it at first, and then elbowed him off, which he thought highly amusing. Things very gradually went from bad to worse.

Then he got really out of control one day. It was before a holiday and we had a celebration in the company. He had a few drinks, and it ended up with him chasing me out of the office and into the ladies loo. By that time I was really very upset and very irritated, and I kneed him in the balls.

I wish I had done it earlier, because it did bring tears to his eyes, and he disappeared for a long time and came back very subdued.

But then I realised it was never going to be any different, and when I got back after the holiday I handed my notice in. In those days it was easy to get another job.

99

Dawn was a nineteen-year-old secretary in a City stockbroking firm. She was the only woman in an office with twenty-five men. Light-hearted banter soon became harassment.

One clerk, named Anthony, invited her out. She said: 'I flatly refused, and from then on his comments became much more nasty. He began to call me a "tart" and told everyone I "slept around" and was "easy" – all despicable lies.'

Dawn complained to her superior, to no effect. Then the rest of the office turned on her. She said, 'I just couldn't take it any more. I dreaded work, couldn't sleep at night.'

To teach Anthony a lesson, she poured a few drops of Tipp-Ex thinner into his milk 'to make it taste yucky'. What she didn't realise is that Tipp-Ex thinner is deadly poisonous. He spat out the mixture, but still had to be rushed to hospital.

Dawn was instantly sacked, and ended up at the Old Bailey, charged with 'maliciously administering poison to endanger life'. Fortunately for her, the judge – a woman – let her off with a warning and a conditional discharge. By this time, she had found another job.[65]

A health service worker replied to a trade union survey that a harasser had made her want 'to kick the shit out of him'. When asked what action she took, she said, 'One day I did kick the shit out of him!'

Clearly it is much better to try and put a stop to harassment at an early stage, and in a calm way, before you get so upset that you can't control your reactions.

BE POSITIVE

It is rarely easy to tell a harasser to back off, not least because many women are trained to please people and not to cause a stir.

Women who have great difficulty making their feelings or wishes known might consider going to assertiveness classes. These are often run by adult education institutes, and aim to teach women to be more confident and deal more effectively with other people, whether at work or at home.

How easy it is to say something depends not just on your personality. More important is whether the harasser is senior, equal or junior, and also exactly what kind of harassment is involved.

ASKING THEM TO STOP

Telling them off – either jokily or sharply – sometimes works and sometimes doesn't.

'Of those who asked the harasser to stop (fifty-six in all), just over a third said it made no difference, a third said it made the situation better, and just under a third said it made the situation worse.' A trade union survey of health service workers

'There's a presenter who kept asking me out to lunch. I tried joking and said, "Come off it, Fred. You're a married man." But then he said, "Oh, so you *are* interested!" Then I talked to a few other people and discovered he was doing the same thing to them. They said, "You have to be sharp with him." So I was, and he hasn't bothered me again.' Hilary, radio producer

'My previous boss always used to refer to me as a girl. I told him I found it really patronising, and that he wouldn't introduce a new man in the office as "the new marketing boy". He couldn't believe I was saying it! But he stopped calling me a girl.' Shahnaz, editorial assistant

'My boss grabbed my hand and pressed it to his trouser flies – he had an erection. I told him to "piss off". He said I had ideas above my station in life.' A technician[66]

'I came into work one day and saw that someone had pinned up a girlie calendar. My first reaction was one of amazement – it was in the typing pool where it was all women! It turned out the calendar belonged to my boss, the only man in the office. When I insisted he take the poster down, he leered and asked me if I was frigid. He kept on about how I should be proud of my lovely figure.' Amanda, typist[67]

DIRECT ACTION

Some women take direct action at the first sign of harassment. But it is unwise to do this unless you feel comfortable and confident about it.

> **66**
> *My boss patted me on the bum in front of a group of people, so I patted him on the balls. He went bright pink and he never did it again.*
> **99**
>
> Alice, graphic designer

'I introduced the harasser to a six-foot-tall supposed boyfriend.' A health service worker[68]

'A reporter smacked me on the bottom – he was a famous mauler. I hit him round the head with a newspaper. There were a few witnesses. It didn't happen again.' A TV news production assistant[69]

'An electrician put his arms round me, and when I tried to move away, he held me tighter. I threatened to knee him in the balls, and raised my knee. He removed his arms and expressed amazement at my reaction.' A researcher[70]

Whether you can do things like this depends very much on who the harasser is. Obviously, it's much easier to whack an equal than the managing director!

66

If one of the waiters slaps me on the bottom, I slap him right back. But it's not so simple when it's the head waiter.

99

Marie, waitress

PUTTING IT IN WRITING

You may find it easier to write to the harasser, rather than speak to him in person. If so, you should always keep a copy of the letter, first for yourself, and second in case you need to take matters further. You could then use the letter as evidence that you have already raised the issue with the harasser.

Women Against Sexual Harassment (WASH) say:

66

Our experience is that most people – if you put the option to them – will choose to write rather than say something.

'It works more successfully and it's considerably less painful. It's less likely to lead to conflict – it's hard to argue aggressively with a letter. And you retain some level of control over the situation.

'Also you can be constructive, in a way that you may not feel able to be face-to-face.

99

A sample letter of complaint:

Dear ....

    I am writing to complain about what you (did/said) to me on (date/yesterday/this morning), when you ....
(Over the previous months you have ....)

    I want you to stop this behaviour now/I want you to stop calling me .... I find this offensive and unacceptable.

    I am keeping a copy of this letter and shall take further action if you do not stop immediately.

Yours sincerely,

KEEPING A DIARY

It is wise to keep a diary of events. You can note down the time and place of each incident of harassment, and what exactly he or they said or did.

You can also note how the harassment made you feel, and whether your health has suffered. And if you do have health problems, and need to visit your doctor, keep a note of it.

Kathy is a young ambulance assistant. Her supervisor, an ambulance driver in his sixties, began harassing her. He assaulted her in a lift. She reported the incidents to management and her union rep, but they told her 'all ambulancemen are like that'.

Kathy got very depressed and went to her doctor, who took one look at her and asked what on earth was wrong. Kathy explained her situation, and the doctor told her she was being sexually harassed at work, and that if she had no help locally, she should contact the union official for the region. She did this, and finally found a woman union rep who took up her case.

TAPE-RECORDING

Some people, who had the skills and opportunity, have secretly tape-recorded conversations with the harasser.

Karen took legal action against an engineering company after she was harassed by one of the directors. He denied her allegations, but because she happened to have taped one of his conversations with her, the industrial tribunal believed her account of events rather than his.

PIN-UPS

Nudity has different meanings in different cultures. In western Europe, it signals sexual availability or vulnerability.

If people put up pin-ups in your workplace, you can:

✳ Ask them politely to take them down. Point out, if necessary, that you dislike them and that they are offensive and demeaning

✳ Ask someone from your union or management to get them taken down

✳ Take them down yourself

✳ Put up pictures of naked men.

It is obviously best if men can be persuaded to take the pin-ups down themselves. If they refuse, a swift way to bring them to their senses – if you are brave enough, and preferably have colleagues to back you up – is to put up pictures of naked men.

Men are not used to seeing idealised naked versions of themselves displayed for female consumption, and it makes them profoundly uncomfortable.

You could start a discussion about why pin-ups are offensive to women. You could ask:

✳ Do you put them up in your living-room at home?

✳ How would you feel if there were pictures of naked men all over the place?

You could point out that pin-ups are offensive because:

✳ They represent women as sex objects for public consumption

✳ By putting them up, men emphasise that a workplace is a male place, and that women workers do not belong there.

The best solution is to get management to make a policy that pin-ups are not appropriate in the workplace.

UNIONS

Your union representative – if you are in a union – may be a good person to turn to early on if you have a problem. The rep can report your problem to management, and if management fails to take effective action, your union may support you in taking your case to a tribunal. If your workplace representative is reluctant to help you, you can try a full-time official.

When Sarah was harassed by the manager of a supermarket in Scotland, she reported the problem to her USDAW shop steward. The steward hesitated at first about doing anything because she was worried about her own position. But eventually she reported the harassment both to a regional manager and to the USDAW area organiser. He advised her to get a written statement from Sarah, which she did.

The USDAW organiser also immediately contacted management, arranged a meeting and requested an immediate investigation. A personnel manager interviewed first Sarah (who was accompanied by her shop steward) and then the harasser.

The company severely reprimanded the harasser, but did not move him from the store. Instead, they offered to move Sarah.

She resigned and, supported by USDAW, went to a tribunal claiming constructive dismissal. Another young woman gave evidence in her support.

The tribunal criticised management's handling of the incident, and awarded Sarah £3,794 for sex discrimination.

More than 1,300 post office workers went on strike in Oxfordshire and Wiltshire in October 1990 after a cleaner, Yvette, was assaulted by a supervisor, and management failed to act.

Married with two young children, Yvette had only been two weeks in the job when her immediate superior trapped her in a store cupboard, switched off the light, barred her exit and molested her.

She escaped, burst into tears and complained to management. They first moved her to another area of the depot – then, astonishingly, moved him to the same area, where he proceeded to follow her about.

Union approaches to management had no effect. The strike started and left the whole Oxfordshire area without mail for eight days. Eventually the harasser was removed and demoted, and a serious offence mark was put on his records.

Your union can also help combat sexual harassment in other ways.

Many unions now have policies against sexual harassment. You can find out your union's policy by asking your representative or head office for copies of its publicity leaflets and statements on sexual harassment. Some unions also cover the issue in their papers or magazines.

Trade unionist Maureen O'Mara of Unison says:

66

It's an issue that's vastly under-reported. Many women say nothing because they don't want to lose their jobs.

'We have cases all over the country – a nurse harassed by a consultant, a theatre nurse assaulted by an anaesthetist, women ambulance crews harassed by men, a young Asian nursing auxiliary in a home for the mentally handicapped assaulted by a male nurse.

'Organisations may have policies against sexual harassment, but what they don't do is say to their managers, "This is a serious issue – you must train your staff and tell them that this is unacceptable." It's the difference between having statements at national level, and management actually taking them seriously.

99

Unions also:

* Issue publicity leaflets and pamphlets explaining what sexual harassment is and how to combat it

* Try to get managements to set up procedures to deal with complaints of sexual harassment

✱ Organise training sessions for union representatives and officials, to help them handle sexual harassment cases

✱ Pay for lawyers to represent members in tribunal cases.

COUNSELLORS

Increasingly, unions are setting up networks of counsellors – also known as 'sympathetic friends' or 'sympathetic listeners' – whom you can turn to first if you are being sexually harassed.

You can tell a counsellor about your problem, and she (they are usually women) will listen in a supportive way. She will then advise you on the courses of action you could take:

✱ If, having discussed the problem, you decide to do nothing – you might wish to come back to the counsellor later – that is fine. But remember that if ever you decide to take legal action, you have to apply to an industrial tribunal *within three months* of the last incident of harassment.

✱ If you decide to tell the harasser to stop – either in person or in writing – you can discuss how to do this with the counsellor, and then come back to her to talk about what happened.

✱ If you decide the matter should be reported to management, or if you want to take legal action, the counsellor will suggest you contact your union rep. You can, however, come back to her at all stages to discuss what is happening.

✱ If your health and well-being have been severely affected by what is happening – or has happened – the counsellor may suggest you go to a doctor or therapist for specialist help. This is needed only in a small number of cases. Usually, being able to talk about the harassment to someone supportive is enough to set a person on the road to recovery.

Counsellors or sympathetic friends are usually volunteers. Unions advertise for them among their membership, and make an initial selection from the applicants. These then attend short training courses and, if they appear to be suitable, become counsellors.

The precise arrangements vary. The banking union BIFU, which is a pioneer in this field, supplies members with a list of counsellors across Britain, giving their work and home addresses and telephone numbers. People can then choose from the list — they might, for instance, prefer someone who works in a different bank from themselves.

Pam Monk of BIFU says:

❝

We did some research and found that sexual harassment problems often come up in different forms from other problems at work. For instance, somebody's had a lot of sick leave, or is perhaps on a disciplinary charge, or behaving in an unusual way. And it turns out that what is at the bottom of it is sexual harassment.

We felt there was a general need for education on the subject, but also that this type of problem needed handling in a specific way.

First, we felt it needed different procedures, because our usual grievance and disciplinary procedures often involve a lot of people in a very adversarial context.

For sexual harassment cases, we try to get employers to set up procedures which will allow the problem to be resolved informally. We want the issue to be handled sensitively, by people who know about sexual harassment. It mustn't be circulated round the whole office.

We also felt that there was a role for specially trained counsellors. We already had our representatives and officials — their role is to put someone's case forward.

But we felt there was also a need for somebody else, whom people could firstly just go to and talk to. Somebody who would listen to them and believe them, and not ask silly questions like, "Did you lead him on?" Somebody who could then say: "If you want to take it any further, these are the various options that are open to you, and this is what will be involved if you do want to take it further."

If the person doesn't want to take it any further, then that's fine. Or if they want to phone up next week and talk again, that's fine too. If they want to take it up with their employer, or take a sex discrimination case, that would be handled by their representative. But they can still speak to their counsellor outside of that, to give them support.

99

COMPANY SERVICES

Some companies are setting up a similar service, sometimes linked to a telephone helpline. However, for some women, it is a problem if the counsellors appear in any way linked to the company. In this case, you may prefer to turn first to an outside agency.

Unfortunately, due to lack of funding, some smaller independent organisations have difficulty coping with all the requests for help that they get. If you leave a message on an answerphone and no one gets back to you, don't despair. Try another organisation (see pages 111–113 for a list of organisations).

OTHER UNIONS

If you are in a union which does not have special sexual harassment counsellors, you may find that your representative at branch level is sympathetic and deals well with your problem. This is most likely to be the case in unions which take time and trouble to educate their members and train representatives.

If your union rep is unhelpful, go to regional level, or if necessary to headquarters. Most unions have an equality officer or women's officer who can advise you. The Trades Union Congress also has officers dealing with how the trade union movement can improve the handling of sexual harassment cases, so you could get in touch with them if your union has not dealt with your case satisfactorily.

Two replies to a health service union survey in 1991 complained about the response of union representatives to sexual harassment cases: 'They just shook their heads and laughed,' and, 'He just laughed and said I shouldn't be so pretty.'

The Manufacturing, Science and Finance Union advises its members to: 'Talk to a union representative as soon as possible. If your workplace representative and Regional Officer are both male, ask your representatives for the name of a woman shop steward or branch/group woman/equality officer, woman committee or executive member to whom you can speak. (Failing local contacts, the National Women's Officer will be pleased to help.)'

When Tracey, a bricklayer, was badly harassed by fellow workers, union representatives at local level would not support her. A tribunal recorded her complaint that 'there was connivance to a certain extent and some participation by some union officials in some of the matters about which she was making complaint'.

But then the UCATT regional representative took up her case, and her experience was quite different. In the tribunal's words, he 'undoubtedly acted with great expedition and great energy on her behalf to put right what she sees are miscarriages of justice'.

Tracey won £15,000 in an out-of-court settlement.

UNION MEMBERS' RIGHTS

Remember – if you are paying your subs, you can expect your union to help you if you are being sexually harassed (or harassed in any way).

By allowing harassment, your employers are breaking their contract to provide you with a safe working environment. Your union is there to protect you from breaches of contract.

These days, too, unions are trying to attract members by showing that they can deal with people's concerns other than the issue of pay.

If you feel your union is not taking sexual harassment seriously, why not press them to do so?

* In your workplace, you could suggest that the union should press management to adopt a policy against sexual harassment.

* You could also suggest a resolution to be debated at the union's annual conference. Unions should be encouraged to ensure that representatives at all levels, as well as officials, are

trained to combat sexism and sexual harassment. Educational material should be provided for all members.

SEXUAL HARASSMENT: UNION LITERATURE

Some unions have produced special leaflets aimed at men, to try to persuade them to change their attitudes.

A leaflet produced by the civil service union, the CPSA, asks men:

'DO YOU

* eye up, leer or stare at, colleagues at work?

* make comments about their bodies, whistle or catcall at them?

* touch, pinch, caress or hug your colleagues?

* make sexual advances to other people at work?

* take advantage of your position to pressurise colleagues for dates and/or sexual favours?

* display sexually explicit material, such as pin-ups from newspapers, calendars or magazines?

'Are you sure the people on the receiving end of this treatment welcome it? You may try to fool yourself that it is only "a bit of harmless fun" or even flattering, but it may not be seen that way by your victims. They will at best be bored by your behaviour and at worst find it degrading and threatening.'

HARASSER IN THE UNION?

There is, of course, a particular problem if the harasser (or harassers) is in the same union as the person they are harassing. There has, indeed, been at least one case where a woman union official accused another official of harassing her, and took legal action against the union. Unions differ in how they handle such situations.

The MSF changed its rules in 1991 to allow the immediate suspension from union office of any member accused of sexual harassment, pending the outcome of an investigation.

Some unions will not provide legal representation for members accused of sexual harassment, while others will (on the grounds that a person is innocent till proven guilty).

At least one union – the print union, GPMU – has taken the very positive step of assisting a young woman who was not a member, but who was taking legal action against three men who were members.

COMPANY POLICIES

Unions try to get employers to agree to adopt policies and procedures against sexual harassment. **Some employers take sexual harassment seriously, and treat it as gross misconduct, which leads to instant dismissal.**

An employee of Oxford University was dismissed in 1992, and three others were given formal warnings, as a result of the university's new code on sexual harassment.

British Rail and Brighton Borough Council are among the public sector bodies which provide trained counsellors or 'sympathetic friends' to give help and support.

The BBC has set up a telephone helpline, through which people can obtain confidential advice.

One university – Central Lancashire – has a full-time staff member dealing with sexual and other forms of harassment, while other universities have staff acting as counsellors.

But although many companies and organisations, especially in the public sector, have taken at least some steps forward, there has been a woeful lack of action by many employers.

When researchers at the Manchester School of Management investigated the sexual harassment policies of 110 of Britain's top companies, they found that sixty-three per cent had no specified procedure to deal with complaints, nor a specified person to receive complaints. Further, eighty-eight per cent of personnel directors had not issued a policy statement of any kind regarding management's attitude to sexual harassment.

GOOD POLICIES

Good policies and procedures aim to protect employees from some of the hazards and traumas that can follow when they make a complaint about harassment.

Pam Monk of the banking union BIFU says:

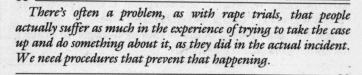

There's often a problem, as with rape trials, that people actually suffer as much in the experience of trying to take the case up and do something about it, as they did in the actual incident. We need procedures that prevent that happening.

The Equal Opportunities Commission for Northern Ireland advises employers to:

✱ Treat complaints of sexual harassment seriously and sympathetically. Where necessary, ensure that a female member of management is available to listen to the woman's grievance.

✱ Enquire discreetly if other workers have similar problems and, if so, take details, ensuring confidentiality at all times.

✱ Discuss with the complainant what action she wishes to be taken and ensure that effective steps are taken to remedy the situation.

✱ With the complainant's agreement, encourage support for her among her work colleagues, and ensure that no victimisation occurs.

London Underground issues a leaflet to employees which advises them what to do in the event of any kind of harassment. The leaflet includes a list of both company counsellors and trade union representatives whom people can contact.

One section, headed 'Resolving a complaint', explains:

'The manager with whom you have lodged your grievance will be responsible for applying the grievance procedure. They will ensure that an investigation is carried out and that all necessary steps are taken to resolve the problem.

'He or she will arrange a fact-finding enquiry. This will involve interviewing the complainant, the alleged harasser and any relevant witnesses. The manager will ensure that no unacceptable cross-questioning occurs.

'A justified complaint can result in disciplinary action and, in extreme cases, dismissal. If the complaint is unsupported, no record will be kept on the alleged harasser's file.

'It is the responsibility of the employing manager to protect the complainant from retaliation.'

BAD PRACTICES

While some companies handle complaints well, others do not. Many women have been subjected to horrendous experiences, including:

* Bullying not just by the harasser, but also by others in the workplace, including women. Such bullying can involve ostracising a person, giving them the worst tasks, or constantly criticising their work.

* Being asked questions during an investigation such as 'Did you lead him on?', 'What were you wearing at the time?' and 'Surely he was only joking?'. Questions like this undermine the complainant by assuming *she* is in the wrong, rather than the person who has harassed her.

* Being referred by a personnel officer to a psychiatrist or therapist, who treats the problem as if it is imaginary, or suggests the woman 'learn to live with it'.

* Being moved to a different area. In harassment cases, the person who has been harassed should *never* be moved (unless they are keen to be). It should always be the harasser who is moved.

✳ Being sacked. Believe it or not, some women are sacked when they complain about a harasser! This has to be the most unjust response of all.

A policewoman said:

66

*When I made a complaint of sexual harassment by a male colleague, I was made to feel that it was **my fault** by a supervisor. Since then I am to be moved to a non-operational role while my offending colleague is being moved to a position of his own choosing, **as the allegations have put stress on him and his family**.*[71]

99

In one case within a television company, a woman who alleged harassment was offered £3,000 to leave her job and drop the allegation.

Many women who take cases to industrial tribunals do so because either they have been sacked after making a complaint, or their life has been made so intolerable that they have felt forced to resign. (See Chapter Four for more information on taking legal action.)

A WELL-HANDLED COMPLAINT

Clare, twenty-one years old, worked in the office at a supermarket. When she went to the loading bay, the manager of that area, a sixty-year-old man, used to put his arms around her and cuddle her.

'This made me feel awkward, but I was too embarrassed to do or say anything,' she said.

He did the same to other young women too.

'After a while,' she continued, 'he started to go further and kissed me on the lips. It started to affect my relationship with my boyfriend – I couldn't bear my boyfriend touching me.'

During a big row with her boyfriend, Clare told him what was happening.

'He demanded the manager's name and said he would go down

and sort him out. I calmed him down and promised I would tell the store manager next day.

'I was very nervous about saying anything to the store manager, so I told my office manager. He asked me if I would like him to tell the store manager, and I said, "Yes".

'That afternoon the store manager called me into his room and asked me to explain the situation. I told him everything and he said he would sort it out.

'He took John into his office and told him he had received a complaint about his behaviour. He did not tell John who had complained, but because I was the only girl he had kissed, John knew that it was me.

'John came up to me and said that if I had told him I didn't like what he was doing, he would have stopped. He said I should not have told the store manager. After things had settled down he treated me with respect and did not come near me, and nothing more was said about it.

'I wish I had done something sooner, but I was very shy and quiet then. I am a much stronger person now and I wouldn't let anyone intimidate me, whoever they were.'

A BADLY HANDLED COMPLAINT

Rose, a sixteen-year-old school leaver, went to work in the bakery department of a major supermarket chain. Years later, she still vividly remembers what happened:

'I was nervous, shy and naïve. The bakery manager was a creepy little man with dirty fingernails and foggy glasses. He never left me alone. Whenever no-one was there, he made disgusting comments with reference to all imaginable sexual acts, some of which I had never heard of at the time. He touched me intimately by surprise, he tried to kiss me, and made gestures whenever no one was looking.

'I was scared stiff. I felt dirty and guilty. After three weeks I confided in a friend, who suggested I tell the manager of the store.

'I asked to see him and told him all. He asked me for the exact words he used, and all the details blow-by-blow. I sat in his office in tears for over an hour.

'At the end his kind expression changed and he suggested I left immediately by my own resignation as "nothing but trouble" would come of it.

'I left thinking I couldn't cope with work or men or the big wide world.

'I coped since, and now at thirty-two know that I would react totally differently in the situation. I *hope* that these days management are more sympathetic to school leavers in this type of situation.'

INAPPROPRIATE RESPONSES

In some cases, ignorance and lack of training leads to totally inappropriate responses. Instead of investigating a complaint, some personnel officers will evade the issue by sending women to therapists or psychiatrists. This places both the blame for the harassment and the responsibility for 'solving' the problem on the woman's shoulders. Women treated this way become, justifiably, frustrated and angry.

Mrs W returned to work as a secretary after her husband died in a car crash, in order to support her two children. Her boss harassed her over a long period – telling her, among other things, that she would not get promotion unless she slept with him.

Mrs W complained to her employer, a London health authority. They sent her to see a psychiatrist in the hospital, who told her to 'go away and learn to cope with this kind of thing'.

But Mrs W pursued the case, with the backing of her union, and was awarded £6,235 by an industrial tribunal. The tribunal also recommended that her boss be suspended until he was found a post in another location.

Ms C, an Asian trade union official, was harassed by another official in the same union. When she complained about the harassment to the union, she was advised to go to a therapist.

The therapist did not want to talk about the harassment, but about how she was brought up. Ms C felt this was entirely irrelevant, and as if the blame was being shifted to her shoulders.

She took legal action, and the union settled out of court for an undisclosed sum.

SEXISM *AND* RACISM

People who have been harassed both sexually and racially may have additional problems when they make complaints.

✱ If they are complaining to a white supervisor about a white person, the supervisor may side with the harasser.

✱ They may be seen as 'complainers' – and therefore not to be taken seriously – because they are complaining about more than one thing.

✱ If they are making a complaint about another black or Asian person, they may find that managers find the issue too hot to handle.

Consequently black or Asian women may find that making a complaint is even more of a struggle for them than it is for white women.

Josina, whose parents are African, got a job in a town hall, working for a local council. Here she was harassed by a much older man, also African.

Josina spoke to a colleague, who advised her to report the matter. The two of them went to the council's women's unit, where they were told, 'I cannot believe that a man of his calibre and status and his longstanding would do this.'

Josina complained to her union, who did nothing. She then made a formal complaint to her head of department. The man was suspended for six weeks, but after an internal disciplinary enquiry he was allowed to return to work – and Josina was moved to another department.

She subsequently discovered that two other women had complained about the same man. She refused to let the matter drop, and at the time of writing has begun legal action.

WORTH COMPLAINING

Whatever the risk that an employer will react badly, it is still worth complaining. As the experience of so many women shows, sexual harassment is not something it is possible to live with. The long-term effects of doing nothing may well be as bad as, or worse than, anything an employer can do. And at least if women fight back, we retain our self-respect.

And again – especially as awareness of the issue grows – we may strike lucky and get our complaint sorted out quickly and efficiently.

OUTSIDE AGENCIES

There are various outside agencies you can turn to for help. The service they provide will vary with:

* The policy and function of the agency

* The money and time they have available

* Who you happen to get on the other end of the phone – if anyone!

Addresses are given at the end of this book (see page 111).

EQUAL OPPORTUNITIES COMMISSION (EOC)

The *Equal Opportunities Commission* covers England, Scotland and Wales (a separate one exists for Northern Ireland, see below). The main office is in Manchester, with regional offices in Glasgow and Cardiff.

The EOC explains its role as 'to ensure effective enforcement of the Sex Discrimination Act and the Equal Pay Act, and to promote equal opportunities between the sexes.'

If you need help or advice with a sexual harassment problem (or, of course, a problem of sex discrimination or equal pay), you can write to the EOC or phone them. At certain times of day they have people ready to give advice to members of the public over the phone. Tell the switchboard you would like advice, and you will be put through to someone who can help, or told what time to ring back.

First of all, they will suggest ways you can deal with the problem yourself. They might, with your agreement, arrange for someone from their casework unit to contact your employer to discuss the problem. Or they might suggest you get in touch with a union representative, or with a local organisation.

If you are considering legal action, the EOC might refer you to a local solicitor or law centre with some knowledge of how to handle sexual harassment cases.

The EOC itself will occasionally fund legal actions for sexual harassment. But it is not likely to do so unless your case is one that could break new legal ground. Shortage of money and its policy priorities mean that the EOC prefers to focus on cases which 'raise important issues of principle' or 'clarify a legal issue'.

The EOC's lawyers will help other lawyers to prepare sexual harassment cases. The EOC also advises employers on setting up policies and procedures to combat sexual harassment.

EQUAL OPPORTUNITIES COMMISSION FOR NORTHERN IRELAND (EOCNI)

The *Equal Opportunities Commission for Northern Ireland* is a separate body from the one in Britain, and is much more likely to take a legal case on a complainant's behalf. The EOCNI has identified sexual harassment as a priority area for action, and assists a substantial number of people taking cases to tribunals.

The EOCNI suggests that you contact them if:

✱ You are unable to report the harassment to your union or employer, or

✱ You have reported the matter but prompt action has not been taken, or

✱ You are being victimised as a result of your complaint.

You can phone or write to the EOCNI. If you phone, you will be put through to an initial enquiry officer who will ask you the details. She will pass this information on to a casework officer, who will make an appointment for you to come in and talk to her.

The casework officer will advise you of the options open to you, and might suggest that the EOCNI, with your consent, take the matter up with your union and employer.

If you think you would like to go to an industrial tribunal, the EOCNI's legal advisers will examine the details and estimate whether your case has a good chance of success. On the basis of the legal advice, the EOCNI will decide whether or not it is going to fund your case.

COMMISSION FOR RACIAL EQUALITY (CRE)

The *Commission for Racial Equality* may be able to help you if you are being harassed in both a racist and a sexist way.

Like the Equal Opportunities Commission, they are short of funds and selective about the legal cases they take on. But sometimes both organisations will team up and take a case together.

If you bring a complaint to the CRE, you will automatically be seen by a complaints officer. He or she will then prepare a file, and may make various enquiries, to your employer for instance. The complaints officer then makes a recommendation to the CRE's legal committee as to whether or not they should proceed with the case. About half the complaints brought to the CRE are not proceeded with. They may, however, be able to refer you to another organisation which can help you.

The CRE does not have any facilities for informally chatting about problems, but they will refer you elsewhere if necessary.

When policewoman Sarah Locker, who is of Turkish descent, went to an industrial tribunal alleging sexual and racial harassment, she was backed by both the Equal Opportunities Commission and the Commission for Racial Equality.

A policeman had given Sarah a 'spoof' letter which was supposed to be application by her for specialised training. It said, among other things: 'A few of them courses is right up the street of a third world effnic girl like me . . . I could really go for that Rape and Serious Sexual Offences bit – if they got some nice greasy Mediterrean [*sic*] boys there, wiv all the right bits cut off their fings – the practice might come in handy . . . Me being a Turk an all that (well I was born in Stepney but everybody in my family is from one of those sweaty little places) I fink I'd teach them dick heads a fing or two.'[72]

LOCAL ORGANISATIONS

You may want to make your first port of call a *law centre* or a *Citizens' Advice Bureau*. Such organisations, of course, have to deal with a vast range of issues. So while some may have considerable experience of sexual harassment cases, others may not.

An advantage of going to a local organisation is that they may be able to put you in touch with somebody nearby who can help – a solicitor, perhaps, or a women's organisation.

WOMEN'S ORGANISATIONS

Around the country there are quite a few *women's organisations* which may be able to help you.

WOMEN AGAINST SEXUAL HARASSMENT

Women Against Sexual Harassment (usually known as WASH) is the group that has pioneered the campaigning and advice work in this field. They give advice to sexually harassed people (men as well as women), do research and provide training for organisations. They cannot, however, take on your case and represent you at a tribunal. One problem is that they get lots of enquiries every year but have limited staff and small funds.

CITY CENTRE

For office workers (women and men), *City Centre* is a helpful organisation, providing information and advice. It is London-based, but will take calls from elsewhere. Its workers answer the phone in person on weekdays, and have considerable knowledge of sexual harassment. They will provide advice, support and counselling, but will refer you elsewhere if you need representation.

LESBIAN AND GAY EMPLOYMENT RIGHTS

Gays and lesbians can look for advice to most of the above organisations, or to *Lesbian and Gay Employment Rights* (LAGER).

LAGER gives advice on a wide range of issues related to employment. If you are a lesbian or a gay man experiencing problems at work related to your sexuality, LAGER can give you advice, support and information. This could include things like referring you to a sympathetic lawyer, writing to your employer, or helping you through disciplinary procedures. They generally answer the phone in person, but sometimes need to put the answerphone on. At your request, they will return your call in a way that does not reveal who they are to whoever picks up the phone.

John worked in a factory. Two other workers discovered that he was gay and started to call him abusive names, such as 'queer' and 'poof'. One reportedly said he would like to 'do that fucking poof in'. The other told the foreman he did not want to work with John because he was 'queer' – and the foreman agreed with him.

John contacted LAGER, who wrote a letter for John to give to his employer and to his union representative. The union and the employer told the two workers that they would face disciplinary action if they continued to harass John.

LAGER comments: 'This case ended successfully, but many do not.'

IF SOMEONE NEEDS YOUR HELP

And finally – maybe it's not you but somebody else who is being sexually harassed.

If someone comes to you and tells you she or he is being harassed, it is most important to listen sympathetically to what they say and show that you believe them.

If you are dismissive, they are likely to clam up and won't tell you the whole story.

Remember – telling the story is, for all of us, an important step on the way to solving the problem. It helps us to understand what is happening to us. It helps us to realise we are not the only ones. It helps us to think about what to do next.

**If someone wants help to counteract sexual harassment —
give it to them. No questions asked. Don't stand by if you see
someone being tormented.**

In some situations it is quite clear that you should intervene.

Marina a woman civil servant, was resented by her seniors
because she had financial control over the group, and had the
authority to say whether projects could go ahead.

Their hostility came out very publicly at the Christmas lunch.
Marina said: 'There were twelve people at the meal, and I was the
only woman. It started with them telling dirty jokes. Then they
took the mickey because I am a vegetarian. They obviously knew
that I had asked people to take down pin-ups, because they
started joking about what they would like to see on the department's new calendar. It got cruder and cruder — gang bangs, the
treatment of black women abroad. It was all designed to make me
feel and look small.

'It was eleven to one, and I had only one slight ally. He didn't
say anything at the time but later told me he thought it was
disgusting. He was the most junior there, and felt he couldn't say
anything.'

When helping others, you should make sure that whatever you
do has the consent of the person being harassed. Don't, for
instance, rush off and make complaints on the person's behalf
without asking her first. Let her stay in control of events.

Frank, assistant manager of a small company, saw Geoff, a
young member of staff, repeatedly touching a colleague, Janet.
She was clearly embarrassed by it, but hadn't said anything.

Frank asked Janet, 'Would you like me to have a word with
him?'

She said, 'Oh please, would you? I don't like to.'

Frank said to Geoff, 'I've noticed you touch Janet a lot, and she
doesn't like it. It's sexual harassment, so would you please stop it.'

Geoff replied, 'Oh, I didn't realise she didn't like it.' He didn't
do it again.

FOUR

Using the law

You may decide that the only way to end the harassment, or to gain some financial compensation for what you have endured, is to take legal action.

If you are thinking of legal action, you should definitely consult someone – or some organisation – with expertise in the area, such as the Equal Opportunities Commission or your trade union's women's officer or equality officer. Your local law centre may or may not have experience of sexual harassment cases.

To help you understand the process, this chapter outlines how tribunals and courts work, and the different laws and procedures involved. Of course, for more information relevant to your particular case, you would need to contact a lawyer. Taking a case is a complex matter, and it would be unwise just to approach 'any old solicitor'. You need someone who knows what they are doing!

You might consider legal action in circumstances such as these:

* The harasser refuses to stop

* Your union (if any) and employer do nothing to resolve the problem

* Your employer offers an impossible 'solution', such as moving you instead of the harasser

* You are being victimised after having made a complaint

* You have felt forced to leave the job by the harassment and lack of action by your employer

* You have been sacked.

Most cases are resolved without actually going to court.

Taking legal action should be seen as a last resort, because the process is long and can be very stressful. You will need support from friends and family.

Because it imposes such tremendous burdens on women, the system for hearing sexual harassment cases is definitely in need of reform.

For some women, however, the outcome of legal action is very positive.

Jenny, a manager with a major cleaning company, was persistently harassed by her regional manager. He kept phoning her and continually booked them into the same hotel because he believed 'there was a special chemistry between them'. She complained, and was dismissed after three months with the company.

Backed by the Equal Opportunities Commission, Jenny took legal action. An industrial tribunal awarded her the maximum compensation of £10,000, plus her legal costs.

Jenny said she was 'elated' by this result. She said: 'My message to other women – and men – is that you should never let people walk all over you. Don't let this happen because there are ways you can challenge it.'[73]

But time and again, women who have taken legal action testify to the pain it caused them – although those who win often feel it was worth it in the end.

Marina, a civil servant, went to a tribunal after being bombarded with sexist comments – such as 'You should be at home doing housework' – and crude jokes by several men. She said: 'The tribunal was a farce. The men were never questioned. My independent witness was never questioned. The tribunal chair, a man in his fifties said, "This is the sort of thing we see on Benny Hill, surely that can't offend you – but maybe that's because I am a man."

'He threw out the case on the third day. In his summing up, he called me a liar and said I was frivolous and vexatious. There was no justice. The case was not really tried at all.'

<u>TRIBUNALS</u>

Most sexual harassment cases go to industrial tribunals, though a few go to the county court or the High Court (see page 106). Industrial tribunals are courts designed to sort out disputes between employers and employees. **People go to industrial tribunals when they are alleging sex discrimination and unfair dismissal.**

Such cases are taken under the Sex Discrimination Act and, where unfair dismissal is involved, the Employment Protection (Consolidation) Act.

An industrial tribunal consists of three people who will hear your case. There is a chairman (even the women prefer to be called chairmen!), plus two 'wing members'.

The chair is a barrister or solicitor, while the wing members are not legally qualified. One wing member is meant to represent the employers, and is chosen by civil servants from nominees put forward by employers' organisations, such as the Confederation of British Industry or Chambers of Commerce. The other wing member represents employees, and is chosen by civil servants from people nominated by trade unions.

At the time of writing, in 1993, chairmen are paid £239 per day, while wing members get £110 per day.

Industrial tribunals are organised by three separate offices, one each for:

* England and Wales

* Scotland

* Northern Ireland

Who chooses the members varies slightly in each area.
In England and Wales:

* Chairmen are appointed by the Lord Chancellor (he is head of the legal system and is appointed by the government)

* Wing members are appointed by the Secretary of State for Employment

In Scotland

✱ Chairmen are appointed by the Lord President of the Court of Session (the head of the Scottish legal system)

✱ Wing members are appointed by the Secretary of State for Employment

In Northern Ireland

✱ Full-time chairmen are appointed by the Lord Chancellor and part-time chairmen are appointed by the local Department of Economic Development

✱ Wing members are appointed by the Department of Economic Development

TIME LIMIT

It is most important to know that your application to a tribunal must be made within three months of the last incident of harassment. If you apply after the time limit, you may still be able to get your case heard, but this is at the discretion of the tribunal. So it is always best to try to get your claim in on time.

If you are very close to the time limit, you – or your lawyer – can, as a last resort, send a fax to the Central Office of the Industrial Tribunals (see Useful addresses, page 111). The fax must include:

✱ Your name and address

✱ Your employer's name and address

✱ A statement that you want to take a case of sexual harassment.

If possible you should use the proper form. This is titled 'Application to an Industrial Tribunal' and is known as the IT1, or 'originating application'. It is available from job centres, Citizens Advice Bureaux, or law centres.

THE SEX DISCRIMINATION ACT

The Sex Discrimination Act makes it illegal for a person to discriminate against a woman by:

* Treating her, on the ground of her sex, less favourably than he would treat a man

* Dismissing her, or subjecting her to any 'detriment' – this means putting her under a disadvantage.

Under the SDA, employers can be held responsible for acts of sexual harassment by their employees. Women alleging sexual harassment often take cases against both the employer and the harasser.

The maximum compensation in 1992 was £10,000, but you may get much less. The tribunal calculates the financial losses you have incurred as a result of being harassed. These could include:

* Loss of earnings

* The cost of psychiatric treatment

* The cost of counselling

* Fares to interviews while looking for a new job.

Tribunals may make you an award for 'injury to feelings' (see page 95). This is intended to compensate you for your suffering.

A tribunal may also make recommendations, such as that the employer should move the harasser to another site.

Your lawyer can also ask the tribunal to make an order requiring the employer to train all staff members in how to deal with and prevent sexual harassment.

THE EMPLOYMENT PROTECTION (CONSOLIDATION) ACT

If you have been sacked after sexual harassment, or were forced to resign because of it, you can appeal to a tribunal under the Employment Protection (Consolidation) Act, claiming unfair dismissal.

But you can only use this act *if you have worked for the employer in question for two years full time or five years part time*. (There is no time requirement in cases taken under the Sex Discrimination Act.)

Under this act, employers who allow sexual harassment can be in breach of their contract with you, which includes a general duty of 'mutual trust and confidence'. This means, among other things, that employers have an obligation to treat grievances seriously.

LEGAL REPRESENTATION

There are many finer points of law which we can't go into here – one reason why you should definitely try to have a lawyer to represent you, rather than 'do it yourself'. The law does not just consist of what is written down in acts of parliament, but also of 'case law' – interpretations of the law that have been made in particular cases, and which can be used as precedents.

If you do not have a lawyer, and decide to represent yourself, the tribunal chairman should try to explain the law simply to you.

Heather, a secretary, took a sexual harassment case backed by the Equal Opportunities Commission, who paid for her lawyer – as they do in a handful of cases (see Chapter Three, page 81).

Heather says: 'In the Industrial Tribunals Procedure booklet they state that, "there is no requirement for you to have a representative to act for you", and "you may present your case yourself". This is a strange piece of advice, as I was utterly lost when my solicitor and the respondent's counsel were arguing "points of law". I doubt whether I would have progressed past the preliminary hearing without legal representation.'

Another very good reason for having a lawyer is that you are much more likely to win your case than if you don't. A study of sexual harassment cases showed that sixty per cent of those with lawyers won their cases, while only twenty per cent of those without lawyers did so.[74]

Also, you are likely to find that your employer has hired a lawyer, and so will be in a much stronger position than you, if you don't have one.

Again, if you are representing yourself, you will find yourself in the difficult position of cross-examining the person who harassed you, and may even have indecently assaulted you.

FINANCIAL ASSISTANCE

The government provides money known as 'legal aid' to help people short of money to pay for lawyers. There are strict rules about who is eligible.

But legal aid in tribunal cases is available only for advice and assistance, and not to pay a lawyer to argue your case in court. You may, however, be able to get legal aid for representation if you go to the county court or High Court (see page 106).

You may be entitled to some free legal advice and assistance under the 'green form scheme' (named after the colour of the form you have to fill in to get it). This covers things like drafting your application to the tribunal, writing letters for you, and telephone negotiations.

Because there is no legal aid for representation at tribunals, you need to look elsewhere for free legal representation. You may be able to get support from an organisation which will pay for your solicitor and, possibly, barrister.

Organisations which may be willing to pay for a lawyer include trade unions, law centres and the Equal Opportunities Commission for Northern Ireland. The Equal Opportunities Commission (covering England, Scotland and Wales) and the Commission for Racial Equality will occasionally take cases – generally if they think the case will break new legal ground.

A charity which helps people who can't afford lawyers is the Free Representation Unit (FRU) in London. You can only go to them if you have been referred by another agency. The FRU will try to find a volunteer to represent you. Their volunteers are mainly law students or just-qualified barristers, who take cases for no pay in return for the experience they gain. The FRU gives them a short training. You may get someone kind and keen, but with very little experience of dealing with sexual harassment cases.

FILLING IN FORMS

The process of going to a tribunal starts, inevitably, with filling in forms. If you have a lawyer, she or he will supply the forms and help you to complete them. If you want to get the official information on industrial tribunals yourself, you can get the application form and various booklets free from any employment office, job centre or unemployment benefit office.

* Probably the first form you will fill in is the 'green form', to claim some free legal advice and assistance.

* Next you would fill in a form titled 'Application to an Industrial Tribunal', which requires basic details about yourself, your employer and your complaint. This is also known as the IT1 or 'originating application'.

The organisation Women Against Sexual Harassment has produced a very clear booklet, aimed at lawyers and advice agencies, titled *Sexual Harassment at Work: A guide to legal action*. This explains all the steps a lawyer needs to take, including filling in forms and handling a tribunal hearing.

THE SD74

If you are making a complaint under the Sex Discrimination Act (see page 91), you can fill in a form called the SD74. This is a questionnaire which your lawyer will send to the respondent or respondents (the company and individuals you are complaining about).

On the questionnaire, you give the basic details of your complaint, and you can ask for material such as your complete personnel file and the company's equal opportunities policy. You can also ask questions of the respondent or respondents, querying why they had done certain things in relation to you, for instance: 'Why was it thought necessary that I should accompany the Managing Director, Mr Jones, on a two-day visit to London in December 1992?'

The employer's answer to the questionnaire may make you decide not to take action after all. In this case, your lawyer simply writes to the tribunal to say you wish to withdraw your application.

<u>AWARD FOR INJURY TO FEELINGS</u>

In some cases, your lawyer may suggest that you could be awarded more money for 'injury to feelings' if you can provide evidence of the emotional damage you have suffered. To get an expert opinion, you could see a psychiatrist, who would interview you and assess the effect that the harassment has had on your life. She would then write a report which would be used in your support at the tribunal or court.

Psychiatrist Dr Gillian Mezey says:

66

When people who are involved in a legal case come to see me, they come to the outpatient department at the hospital. I see them individually, and usually it takes about two hours.

'Sometimes I also like to talk to people very close to the woman. Not because I don't believe her, but because sometimes women under-estimate the problems they've got. For instance I saw one woman's husband, and he told me she was waking up screaming at night, which she hadn't thought was relevant.

'The two hours are spent not just talking about the harassment, but also getting to know the woman a bit. It affects different women in different ways. You have to understand what their lives were like before the harassment in order to see how it has affected them.

99

If you are referred to a psychiatrist in these circumstances, it does *not* mean you are mentally ill. Very few women are so severely affected by sexual harassment that they need psychiatric treatment.

Dr Mezey says:

66

Women do have extraordinary coping resources, and I think that the support of other women who actually understand what they have been through is often enough.

I think it would be very useful if there was some kind of self-help support network, which doesn't exist at the moment, where women could discuss their experiences with other women who have been harassed. It would show the woman that she is not alone, that it happens to a lot of women, and that the feelings she has – that she is going completely mad and can't cope – are feelings that other women have had and have managed to cope with, and have got over.

99

TRIBUNAL HEARINGS

Your experience of a tribunal may vary greatly depending on where you live. In all areas, you will have to wait at least several months for your hearing to begin. You could first have a preliminary hearing. Then comes the full hearing, which could last several days. These might not be all together.

Officials make an estimate of how long your case will take – based on factors such as how many witnesses are likely to be called – and allocate a certain number of days. If the estimate proves wrong, and there is not enough time to complete the hearing, it could restart months later.

Buchi's case went through relatively quickly. She applied in April, and the first day of the hearing was held in December. That day, the tribunal listened to her evidence and the respondent's evidence. There was not enough time to complete the hearing, so it continued three months later, in March. That day, the tribunal heard the witnesses and came to a decision. It found Buchi's case 'not proved'.

If you are unlucky, your hearings could extend over months or, if there is an appeal, even years.

Heather found the delays in her case worrying and frustrating. She said: 'The tribunal first set a date for November. The respondent couldn't attend then, so it was put back to December. 'The tribunal then found their office would be closed, so the hearing was put back to March. And then we only had a part hearing – I and all my witnesses were heard, and one of the respondent's witnesses, and then the case was adjourned for six months.

'The case was heard in September, but the chairman was taken ill the following week and we had to wait four months for the result.'

After all that, Heather lost her case and decided to appeal.

APPEALS

If you lose your case, you might want to appeal. If you win, the respondents might want to appeal. Whoever loses at that stage might want to appeal again. Appeals can only be made on points of law. In England, Scotland and Wales, appeals are made first to the Employment Appeal Tribunal (EAT). This consists of a High Court judge and two lay members, one representing workers and the other representing employers. Hearings are held in London or Edinburgh.

If you lose at the Employment Appeal Tribunal, you could appeal again:

* In England and Wales, you would go to the Court of Appeal

* In Scotland, you would go to the Court of Session

* In Northern Ireland, there is no Employment Appeal Tribunal. Instead, appeals are made direct to the Northern Ireland Court of Appeal, which consists of three High Court judges.

Jean Porcelli's case was a legal landmark: it established that sexual harassment is illegal under the Sex Discrimination Act.

But Mrs Porcelli had to go through three hearings before she won. She lost at the industrial tribunal, then again at the Employment Appeal Tribunal. Finally the Scottish Court of Session – the equivalent of the English Court of Appeal – ruled in her favour.

GATHERING EVIDENCE

If you have any witnesses who will support your account of events, your lawyer will arrange for them to come along and give evidence. You might, for instance, have a colleague who saw or heard one of the incidents of harassment, or a colleague who was harassed herself by the same person.

Your evidence could include:

✳ Witnesses, perhaps colleagues from work, or people from home who have seen how the harassment has affected you. It is best if they can give their evidence in person, but if they can't, they can supply a statement.

✳ Expert witnesses, for example a psychiatrist's report on the damage done by the harassment to your well-being

✳ Your harassment diary, giving details of everything the man or men said and did to you, and how you responded

✳ Your personnel file, and other information you may have extracted from your employer

✳ Letters to or from you which are relevant to the case

✳ Any tape-recording you may have made of the harasser in action.

Evidence presented on paper will be put together in what is called a 'bundle'.

Tribunals do not require the same standard of evidence as criminal courts. In criminal courts, the evidence has to be 'beyond reasonable doubt'. But a tribunal can make a decision based on the 'balance of probabilities'.

You must make sure that your lawyer has every piece of information that might be useful. Don't be shy of mentioning things. Don't assume that she or he will ask you the right questions. Try to remember everything the harasser did or said to you.

Think about the people that the harasser may bring as witnesses, and what you know about their relationship with him. He may, for instance, try to undermine you by bringing as witnesses other women from your workplace. Sometimes women are too worried about their jobs to refuse. On more than one occasion, a harasser has called as a witness a woman with whom he is having an affair!

As part of the process of collecting information, your lawyer may need to ask you embarrassing questions, for instance, 'Did you ever fancy the man who harassed you?' Even if you did, you can still take a case for sexual harassment – the fact that you once fancied him does not give him the right to harass you.

Your lawyer has to make decisions about the best way to bring this kind of information out – or whether to bring it out at all.

Debbi King, a barrister who works for a law centre and often handles sexual harassment cases, explains:

> **66**
>
> *When I take a statement from a woman, I get it typed up and send her a draft to correct or amend if necessary. The statement doesn't go before the tribunal – it is just for my benefit as her representative.*
>
> **99**

THE PRESS

Before the tribunal hearing, you should discuss with your lawyer the best way to handle the press.

In some parts of the country, especially London, there is considerable press interest in sexual harassment cases – usually for all the wrong reasons. In the morning, reporters comb through the lists of cases coming up that day, and pick out the ones being taken under the Sex Discrimination Act.

You may well find that there are reporters from news agencies and papers in the courtroom, and even photographers hanging around outside. Agency reporters may write quite factual accounts – but these are sold to newspapers, which may completely rewrite them, picking out the 'juicy' details to titillate their readers.

PRESS HARASSMENT

Valerie, an agency reporter, says:

> **66**
>
> *The agency wants us to cover sexual harassment cases because the papers want to buy those stories, so the agency makes money from them.*
>
> *I would prefer not to put the salacious details in my reports, but I have to, because other news agencies are also covering the*

cases, so I'd get into trouble if I didn't report everything.

*'Sometimes my editor even asks me, "Has she got big breasts?
Will she make a good picture?"*

99

Reporters may come up and talk to you in the applicants'
waiting room or in the corridor. You should decide in advance
whether or not you are going to talk to them yourself, or whether
it would be better for your lawyer to make a statement on your
behalf. Or perhaps you would prefer no comment to be made to
the press at all. Publicity can be a double-edged sword, as we shall
see later.

A bill going through parliament at the time of writing is likely
to give industrial tribunals the power to restrict media coverage of
sexual harassment cases.

An amendment to the Trade Union Reform and Employment
Rights Bill proposes that at the request of any party to a case, or
on its own initiative, a tribunal would be able to make a 'restricted
reporting order'. This would mean that, while the media could
still attend hearings, they could not publish anything which
would identify the parties to a case. The Employment Appeal
Tribunal would also be able to make such an order.[75]

Victims of indecent assault and other serious sexual offences are
already protected by the Sexual Offences (Amendment) Act
1992, which makes it an offence to publish reports identifying
them, unless they give their consent to being identified.

In the Republic of Ireland, the media are not allowed into
hearings before the Labour Court – which hears sexual harassment cases – unless one of the parties requests it. The court can
overrule such a request. The result of the case is made public, but
in general terms, without revealing the identities of the parties or
the details. After the decision, however, the parties are free to
speak to the press if they wish.

APPLICANT AND RESPONDENT

As the person who is taking the case, you are described as the 'applicant'. The person you are taking the case against is the 'respondent'.

You will probably be taking a case against two respondents: your employer and the person who harassed you. (In some cases, of course, they are the same person.)

THE TRIBUNAL PROCEDURE

Tribunal procedure resembles court procedure, even though it is more informal. Precisely how informal it is will depend very much on how the chairperson handles the situation.

It is a good idea to visit an industrial tribunal before yours comes up – they are open to the public – so that you can get an idea of what to expect.

When your hearing comes up, you might like to take a friend along with you for support.

You may have to travel quite a way for your hearings. Tribunals for the London area, for instance, are held in either Euston or Croydon.

THE COURT SET-UP

When you arrive, you will be asked to wait in the applicants' waiting-room. The respondents have a separate waiting-room.

The courtroom is less formal than it would be in a county court or the High Court, but it can still feel pretty intimidating.

The three members of the tribunal sit in a row at one end of the room. Their table is on a platform a few inches above the rest of the room. The chairperson sits in the middle. They wear ordinary clothes. Facing them are tables at which the lawyers for the applicant and respondent sit, and the applicant and respondent themselves, if they wish.

Behind them are a few rows of chairs. Here witnesses, friends, the public and the press can sit.

At the side, between the tribunal and the lawyers, is the place where witnesses give evidence. This is usually a table at which they sit.

GIVING EVIDENCE

If your lawyer wishes to make an opening statement, the tribunal will listen to it. This is usually only necessary in complicated cases.

Generally, the hearing begins with you being asked to give evidence. You will go to the witness table, and you will be asked to swear, while standing, that you will 'tell the whole truth and nothing but the truth'. The court clerk will give you a card with the words on it, so that you can read them out. You can either swear on a religious book or, if you prefer, you can 'affirm'.

After that, you can usually sit down to give your evidence. You will be able to see the bundle of documents which the tribunal has in front of it, if you need it to refer to it.

Then your lawyer will ask you questions. She or he is not allowed to ask you questions which 'lead' you in a particular direction, such as, 'It was Mr Jones who squeezed your breasts at the firm's party, wasn't it?' Instead, she or he could ask, 'Did anyone touch you at the firm's party?'

Once you have started giving evidence, if there are any lunchbreaks or adjournments, you are not allowed to discuss your evidence with your lawyer or anyone else until you have finished giving evidence.

QUESTIONING

After your lawyer has questioned you, the respondent's lawyer may do so. The chair and wing members of the tribunal may also question you, to try to clarify the situation. The respondent, your witnesses and his witnesses will also be questioned.

When the respondent's lawyer questions you, it is known as 'cross-examination'. You may find this difficult and distressing. The respondent is likely to throw at you everything he can think of.

His lawyer may try to ask you about your sex life or what kind of clothes you wore to work. Your lawyer should be ready to challenge irrelevant questions: your sex life is your own business, and just because you have slept with one or more men, does not give other men the right to harass you. Nor does the kind of clothes you wear give them the right to harass you.

Another thing you may find difficult is being in the same room as the man or men who harassed you.

Sometimes, when a woman is giving evidence, the harasser stares at her continuously. If this happens, you can complain to the tribunal that he is deliberately making you uncomfortable.

Debbie, a receptionist, was one of only two women working in a firm with forty men. The harassment began as soon as she started the job.

They would say things like, 'Get your knickers off!' and make offensive gestures. One man dropped a coin down the front of her blouse, then put his hand down to try and retrieve it. Another put his hand up her skirt.

She told them to stop, to no avail. When she complained to the manager, he said she should tell them to 'fuck off', but she is a shy person, and didn't want to do so. The next time she complained the manager sacked her on the spot.

Debbie was disturbed, angry and depressed. She decided to take legal action, and found the tribunal was an ordeal too. All the harassers were there, and their solicitor asked her, 'How many men have you slept with?' Luckily her solicitor jumped in and pointed out that it was an irrelevant question, which she did not have to answer.

Debbie was awarded over £4,000, but had to go back to court to force the company to pay up.

> 66
>
> *I have seen applicants reduced to tears in the witness box.*
>
> 99
>
> Valerie, court reporter

THE TRIBUNAL RESULT

After all the evidence has been heard, the chairperson will ask the respondent's and the applicant's lawyers to sum up. Then everyone, except the panel deciding the case, leaves the tribunal room.

The tribunal members then get together to make their decision. If you are lucky, they will call everyone back into tribunal the same day, and the chairperson will announce the result. But you might have to wait much longer – several weeks, even – to hear the decision.

The tribunal members will draw up a report. This consists of their decision and recommendations, plus an extensive account of the reasons for the decision. This will include a survey of the applicant's case and the respondent's case, and of the legal arguments put by their lawyers.

The three members of the tribunal may not agree on everything, in which case they will point out that the decision is a majority one rather than unanimous.

Mrs W brought a complaint to an industrial tribunal under the Sex Discrimination Act after she had been sexually harassed for over a year by her boss at a south London health authority. She named both as respondents. Her union, NUPE, paid for her legal representation.

The tribunal made a unanimous decision that the respondents should pay her £6,325 for the injury to feelings she had suffered. They recommended that the harasser be moved to another post where he would not come in contact with her, and that the health authority suspend him until they could arrange such a move. The tribunal also recommended that the health authority should not allow the harasser to work in the hospital where Mrs W worked for as long as she was based there.

But the health authority neither moved the harasser nor paid Mrs W until considerably more pressure had been brought to bear by the union.

WIN SOME, LOSE SOME

One estimate suggests that just over half of those who apply to tribunals claiming sexual harassment win their cases.

Between 1986 and 1990, industrial tribunals decided ninety-seven sexual harassment cases, of which fifty-three were successful. That is a success rate of fifty-five per cent.[76]

If you lose your case, you will obviously feel disappointed and even betrayed. But you should not allow yourself to feel completely undermined.

Many people think that all they have to do is go into court, tell the truth, and they will win. But this is far from being the case. It is quite possible that the person who has harassed you will go into court and lie through his teeth, as may his witnesses. The harasser may also have spent a lot of money getting experienced lawyers.

If his case is very well presented and argued, and yours isn't, the tribunal may choose to believe him and not you.

Buchi, a secretary, told a London tribunal that a manager had tried to kiss her in a lift and had asked her to be his mistress, greatly upsetting her.

The tribunal chose to 'prefer his evidence', partly because the incident happened at lunchtime, and they did not think he would have done such a thing when there were a lot of people moving about. They also doubted Buchi because she was unsure about the date of the incident: in their view she would have remembered the date of such a traumatic event.

How your case is handled may vary greatly, depending on factors such as:

* the particular members of the tribunal

* the quality of the lawyers on both sides

* the area where your case is being heard.

According to the Equal Opportunities Commission for Northern Ireland, the industrial tribunals there 'regard sexual harassment as a very serious issue and have generally therefore approached the conduct of sexual harassment cases in a sympathetic manner, regardless of the final outcome.'

FINANCIAL AWARDS

As has been said, financial awards made by tribunals are not large. The maximum they could award in 1992 was £10,000.

Sometimes awards are very low. This means that you could win, but – even if you have not paid for your lawyer – you could still be considerably out of pocket in terms of the time you have spent pursuing the case.

Karen Wileman won her tribunal case alleging sexual harassment over a period of four-and-a-half years by Mr Atthill, one of the directors of Minilec Engineering.

But the tribunal awarded her only £50 for injury to feelings, plus £100 for victimisation, plus £372 for loss of wages.

OTHER COURTS

Sexual harassment cases can go not only to industrial tribunals but also to the county court or the High Court, and a few do.

If the maximum amount of money a tribunal can award would be too low to compensate you properly, your lawyer might advise you to go to these 'civil courts', as they are called.

The county court and particularly the High Court can award much larger sums, so going to them can be advantageous for high earners who have lost a lot in wages, or for people who have been seriously assaulted.

Also, your lawyer might advise you to go to a civil court if the issues in your case are legally more complex than those usually handled by tribunals. For example, if you have been seriously assaulted or raped, or falsely imprisoned, it would be more appropriate for a civil court to decide the issues.

Another advantage of going to a civil court could be that, if you are eligible, legal aid is available to pay for lawyers to represent you, whereas there is no legal aid for representation in tribunal cases.

To get legal aid, your capital and income would be assessed to see if you qualify for all or part of your costs to be paid. You would also have to show that your case has a reasonable chance of success.

CRIMINAL CASES

If you report the assault to the police, the case could be taken by the Crown Prosecution Service, if they feel there is enough evidence. The harasser could end up with a prison sentence and be ordered to pay you compensation.

Margaret, a twenty-one-year-old receptionist, came from Ireland to London to work for a millionaire showbusiness entrepreneur. He was fifty-five years old and married with four children.

Four days after she started, he summoned her to his office, claiming he needed paper tissues. Then he put his hand under her skirt and forced her to kiss him.

Margaret resigned her job and went to the police. In court, the entrepreneur admitted indecent assault. The judge sentenced him to two months in jail.

SETTLING OUT OF COURT

Many cases taken to tribunals and courts are settled before the hearing. Employers and alleged harassers will offer to settle your case in order to avoid the publicity that will ensue. They will offer you a sum of money that is likely to approach the amount that the court or tribunal would award you. They might even offer you more than a tribunal could award. They may also offer to pay your legal costs.

They are likely to offer to settle on two conditions. First, that they do not admit liability (which means they are not admitting they have broken the law). Second, that you sign a 'confidentiality' clause to say that you won't discuss details about, for instance, the sum you have been paid.

Applicants who agree to settle may feel angry and frustrated that the employer has not accepted liability, since it means there is no public recognition of the wrong that has been done to them. They may also feel they have been 'bought off'.

'Confidentiality' clauses are causing considerable disquiet among people concerned about sexual harassment, as they allow employers and harassers to avoid publicity.

The publicity given to those who are found to have discriminated is a major deterrent to others. In tribunal cases especially, the sums awarded are not large enough to be a serious threat to employers – the threat of publicity is a more effective sanction.

Sally, a £30,000-a-year executive, refused to sign a confidentiality clause as part of a settlement.

She had taken her employers and the man who had harassed her to the High Court for breach of contract, malicious falsehood, and assault and battery. They denied liability, but the employer paid £25,000 for breach of contract plus substantial legal costs a week before the case went to court.

Sally told the *Independent*: 'They dropped in the confidentiality clause right at the last minute with the largest offer. You can't get legal aid on this, so that's very tempting. They wanted me to say I resigned due to a "clash of personalities". But I wanted to be vindicated, to prove I was not just imagining it all. Being able to talk about it afterwards was very therapeutic, and I could counteract rumours that I had been sacked.'[77]

Taken together, the non-admission of liability and the confidentiality clause can allow employers to avoid making changes in the way their organisations deal with sexual harassment, and can allow harassers to evade altering their behaviour.

If you think you might want to make the details of your case public at a later date, you should instruct your lawyer not to accept a confidentiality clause.

While publicity can be a serious deterrent to harassers, and can help women to establish their credibility, the kind of coverage given to sexual harassment cases by the tabloid press can be very distressing.

'*KINKY CHINKY PEEKED AT MY JING JONG*' announced the *Daily Star*'s front page in inch-high letters on 8 August 1989.

The *Daily Star* was reporting – if that's the word – an industrial tribunal case taken against a fifty-year-old acupuncturist by his twenty-nine-year-old former assistant. She alleged that he had constantly sexually harassed her. Then, when she had worked for him for nearly a year, he sacked her. Her health was affected by the harassment. The tribunal awarded her £4,118.

To the *Daily Star*, it was all a big joke. Their story began:

'A Chinese acupuncturist told yesterday how he treated his busty assistant for a virus by measuring between her nipples.'

The paper described the woman, whom it named, as a 'pretty redhead'.

When it comes to the verdict, the tabloids often don't bother to report it.

Heather found the aftermath of her tribunal hearing very difficult. She said:

66

Some of the press coverage was extremely salacious, and many papers printed my address, with the result that we were inundated with calls from perverts. Some of the calls were aimed at my fifteen-year-old daughter. We had to have our number changed and go ex-directory.

99

It is very difficult to challenge accounts given in the press, because there is no shorthand record of tribunal hearings.

The only official record is the chair's notes of evidence. These are only usually produced if the case has to go to the Employment Appeal Tribunal, and there is an order for them to be typed up.

The reasons for the tribunal's decision are, however, always given in writing.

IS IT WORTH IT?

Women who have been through the court or tribunal system can end up with very mixed feelings. On the one hand, even if they lost, they feel they were right to take action. On the other hand, the process can be so painful that it only adds to the traumas they have already suffered.

Heather, who lost her case and is appealing, says:

66

From my experience at the industrial tribunal, I would find it very difficult to encourage any woman to put herself through this long, unpleasant experience.

However, I feel very strongly that women should have the right to have this behaviour, especially in the workplace, stopped.

> *But I feel very bitter and angry about my treatment, and have a very jaundiced view of justice. I think the industrial tribunal system requires some close scrutiny.*

BENEFIT FOR OTHERS

There is no doubt that however painful such cases are for the women who take them, the benefits for the rest of us have been immense. These brave women have made society, through the courts, state that sexual harassment is reprehensible, harmful and unacceptable, and that employers and harassers can be brought to book for it.

Their determination has ensured that employers and would-be harassers must be a lot more wary about their actions. Otherwise, one of these days, they could find themselves in court.

After a judge sentenced her harasser to two months' imprisonment for indecent assault, Margaret told the press:

> *I fought this battle because I didn't want other women to fall victim to this sort of behaviour.*

USEFUL ADDRESSES AND PUBLICATIONS

ORGANISATIONS

Citizens Advice Bureaux
You will find the address of your local Citizens Advice Bureau in the phone book.
Or you could contact:
National Association of Citizens Advice Bureaux
115 Pentonville Road, London N1 9LZ
Tel: 071 833 2181

City Centre
32–35 Featherstone Street, London EC1Y 8QX
Tel: 071 608 1338
City Centre is a good starting point if you are looking for informal advice over the telephone. It is a fairly small organisation providing information and advice to office workers (women and men), but will take calls from people in other kinds of work. They will provide advice, support and counselling, but will refer you elsewhere if you need legal representation.
City Centre publishes a booklet aimed at people designing policies, titled *Tackling Sexism and Sexual Harassment: A guide for changing the workplace*. Contact them for details of price.

Commission for Racial Equality
Elliott House, 10–12 Allington Street, London SW1E 5EH
Tel: 071 828 7022
The CRE also has offices in:
Birmingham: Alpha Tower (11th floor), Suffolk Street Queensway, Birmingham
B1 1TT
Tel: 021 632 4544
Leeds: Yorkshire Bank Chambers (1st floor), Infirmary Street, Leeds LS1 2JP
Tel: 0532 434413
Manchester: Maybrook House (5th floor), 40 Blackfriars Street, Manchester
M3 2EG
Tel: 061 831 7782

Leicester: Haymarket House (4th floor), Haymarket Shopping Centre, Leicester
LE1 3YG
Tel: 0533 517852
Scotland: 100 Princes Street, Edinburgh EH2 3AA
Tel: 031 226 5186
If you have a complaint involving both sexual harassment and racial harassment,
you could go either to the Equal Opportunities Commission or to the
Commission for Racial Equality. They sometimes team up and work together on
such cases. If you have a complaint involving racial harassment and phone the
Commission for Racial Equality, they will make an appointment for you to see a
complaints officer.

Equal Opportunities Commission
Overseas House, Quay Street, Manchester M3 3HN
Tel: 061 833 9244
EOC regional offices:
Wales: Caerwys House, Windsor Lane, Cardiff CF1 1LB
Tel: 0222 343552
Scotland: St Andrew House, 141 West Nile Street, Glasgow G1 2RN
Tel: 041 332 8018
You can write to the Equal Opportunities Commission, or phone them. At certain
times of the day they have people available to talk to members of the public who
telephone. They will send out a pack of information on sexual harassment at your
request. They also give advice to employers and to lawyers.

Equal Opportunities Commission for Northern Ireland
Chamber of Commerce House, 22 Great Victoria Street, Belfast BT2 7BA
Tel: 0232 242752
You can phone or write to the Equal Opportunities Commission for Northern
Ireland. If you phone, you will be put through to someone who can advise you. If
you have a sexual harassment problem, they may make an appointment for you to
come in to see a casework officer. They will send out a pack of information on
sexual harassment at your request. They also give advice to employers and unions.

Law Centres Federation
Duchess House, Warren Street, London W1P 5DA
Tel: 071 387 8570
You may find the address of your local law centre in the phone book. If not, you
can telephone the Law Centres Federation and they will give you the details of
your nearest one. The Federation cannot itself give you advice on your problem.

Lesbian and Gay Employment Rights
St Margaret's House, 21 Old Ford Road, London EC1 9PL
Tel: 081 983 0696 (gay men and general enquiries)
    081 983 0694 (lesbians)

LAGER gives advice to gay men and lesbians on a wide range of issues related to employment. You can contact them if you are having problems at work related to your sexuality. Their workers answer the phone in person whenever possible, but sometimes have to put the answerphone on. They will always call you back – if you want them to return the call in a confidential way, they are happy to do so. They will also advise employers on equal opportunities policies.

National Harassment Network

University of Central Lancashire, Preston, PR1 2BR
Tel: 0772 892253/892512
The National Harassment Network is an information and resource service for professionals, including employers and trade unions. It was set up by the University of Central Lancashire 'to enable professionals engaged in dealing with harassment to meet regularly in order to update knowledge, exchange good practice, discuss particular areas of concern, obtain guidance and receive support'. They publish a newsletter and run conferences and courses.

Scottish Trades Union Congress

16 Woodlands Terrace, Glasgow G3 6DF
Tel: 041 332 4946
If you live in Scotland and find that your union is not giving you all the help you need, you can contact the Secretary of the Women's Committee at the Scottish TUC.

Trades Union Congress

Great Russell Street, London WC1B 3LS
Tel: 071 636 4030
The TUC has published a set of guidelines titled *Sexual Harassment at Work*. This is available for a small charge from their publications department at the above address.
If you are a trade union member and you have a problem with sexual harassment, you should first go to your branch representative, or to a sexual harassment counsellor, if your union provides them. If these routes prove unhelpful, you can try your regional office or national office. Finally, you could contact the Equality and Social Policy Office at the TUC.

Women Against Sexual Harassment

312 The Chandlery, 50 Westminster Bridge Road, London SE1 7QY
Tel: 071 721 7592/7594
You can phone or write to WASH. They can give advice, but cannot take your case on or represent you at a tribunal. They produce various leaflets and have published a guide aimed at lawyers, titled *Sexual Harassment in the Workplace: A guide to legal action*. They charge for booklets, but will send out leaflets free. As well as giving advice to individuals (men as well as women), they do research and provide training for employers.

OTHER PUBLICATIONS

The Department of Employment's booklet, *Sexual harassment in the workplace: A guide for employers*, and copies of a leaflet for employees, are available from: ISCO 5, The Paddock, Frizinghall, Bradford BD9 4HD.

The European Commission's code of practice on sexual harassment, aimed primarily at employers, is available from: HMSO, 51 Nine Elms Lane, London SW8 5DR Tel: 071 873 8409. It is in the *Official Journal of the European Communities*, L 49, vol. 35, 24 February 1992. Its full title is 'Commission recommendation of 27 November 1991 on the protection of the dignity of women and men at work'. The ISBN number is 011969591 X. Contact HMSO for details of price.

The Institute of Personnel Management has produced a *Statement on Harassment at Work*, which aims to advise employers on how to eliminate harassment of all kinds in the workplace. Their address is: IPM House, Camp Road, London SW19 4UX Tel: 081 946 9100.

Preventing and Remedying Sexual Harassment at Work is a manual aimed at employers, written by Michael Rubenstein, who also wrote the report for the European Commission on which their Code of Practice was based. It is expensive, and is available from the publishers: Industrial Relations Services, 18–20 Highbury Place, London N5 1QP Tel: 071 354 5858.

APPLICATIONS TO INDUSTRIAL TRIBUNALS

England and Wales: Central Office of the Industrial Tribunals, 100 Southgate Street, Bury St Edmunds, Suffolk IP33 2AQ
Tel: 0284 762300
Scotland: Central Office of the Industrial Tribunals, Saint Andrew House, 141 West Nile Street, Glasgow G1 2RU
Tel: 041 331 1601
Northern Ireland: Office of Industrial Tribunals and the Fair Employment Tribunal, Long Bridge House, 20–25 Waring Street, Belfast BT1 2EB
Tel: 0232 327666

REFERENCES

1 *The Guardian*, 3 December 1992, 1 February 1993
2 COHSE survey, 1991. All mentions of a 'health service union survey' refer to the COHSE survey. COHSE is now part of Unison
3 *The Independent*, 29 September 1992
4 *The Sunday Times*, 25 June 1989
5 *The Daily Mail*, 27 September 1990
6 *The Times*, 2 December 1992, quoting article in *Woman*
7 Sergeant Rona Anderson, Jennifer Brown, Elizabeth Campbell, *Sex Discrimination in the Police Service in England and Wales*, Police Research Scheme, 1993
8 *British Medical Journal*, 17 October 1992
9 *The Work of Lesbian Employment Rights*, Lesbian Employment Rights, p. 3
10 *The Guardian*, 8 January 1991
11 *Nursing Times*, 25 November–1 December 1992
12 NUPE booklet on sexual harassment
13 Marsha Rowe, introduction to *Spare Rib Reader* (Harmondsworth, Penguin, 1982), p. 15
14 Quoted in Elizabeth Wilson, *What is to be done about violence against women?* (Harmondsworth, Penguin, 1983), p. 174
15 Germaine Greer, *The Female Eunoch* (London, Paladin, 1971), p. 61
16 Catharine A. MacKinnon, *Sexual Harassment of Working Women* (New Haven and London, Yale University Press, 1979)
17 Porcelli v. Strathclyde Regional Council, *Industrial Cases Reports* (1986)
18 Introduction to eds. Amber Coverdale Sumrall and Dena Taylor, *Sexual Harassment: Women speak out* (California, The Crossing Press, 1992), p. 8
19 Toni Morrison, *Race-ing Justice, En-gendering Power* (London, Chatto and Windus, 1993), p. xvii
20 Report of 'Spot the difference', a conference on the future of women in British TV, 14 March 1991
21 *The Times*, 7 April 1989

References

22 John Kremer and Jenny Marks, *Sexual Harassment at Work in Northern Ireland* (Equal Opportunities Commission for Northern Ireland, 1990), pp. 3–4

23 *The Evening Standard*, 15 October 1991

24 In the case of Collins v. Wilcock, *Industrial Relations Legal Information Bulletin 398*, 3 April 1990

25 *Hansard*, 12 March 1986, col. 937

26 *Hansard*, 12 March 1986, col. 939

27 Address to the EC seminar on sexual harassment at work, 7–9 November 1991, The Hague

28 Clare Short, *Dear Clare . . .* (London, Hutchinson Radius, 1991), pp. 65–6

29 Sara Keays, *A Question of Judgement* (London, Quintessential Press, 1985), p. 301

30 Sara Keays, as above, p. 106

31 Sara Keays, as above, p. 145

32 From eds. P. Carter, T. Jeffs and M.K. Smith, *Changing Social Work and Welfare* (Open University Press, 1992), pp. 236–7

33 *The Financial Times, The Independent*, 6 March 1992

34 Quoted in Andrew Tolson, *The Limits of Masculinity* (London, Tavistock Publications, 1977), pp. 89–90

35 The statistics on men and women at work were supplied by the Labour Research Department

36 *The Guardian*, 25 November 1992

37 Julienne Dickey and the Campaign for Press and Broadcasting Freedom London Women's Group, *Women in Focus* (CPBF, London, 1985)

38 James Woodburn, 'Stability and flexibility in Hadza residential groupings', in eds. Richard B. Lee and Irven Devore, *Man the Hunter* (Aldine Publishing Company, Chicago, 1968), p. 107

39 Cited in Barbara Bush, *Slave Women in Caribbean Society* (London, Heinemann, 1990), pp. 113–14

40 Quoted in Barbara Bush, as above, p. 112

41 Essay by Michael Edwardes in *The British Empire*, vol. 2 (London, Ferndale, 1981), p. 189

42 Ronald Hyam, *Empire and Sexuality* (Manchester University Press, 1990), pp. 2–3, 94

43 See Mona Hearn, 'Life for domestic servants in Dublin, 1880–1920', in eds. Maria Luddy and Cliona Murphy, *Women Surviving* (County Dublin, Poolbeg, 1989), pp. 148–179. This includes some information on servants in England.

44 Jan Lambertz, 'Sexual Harassment in the nineteenth century English cotton industry', *History Workshop Journal*, no. 19, spring 1985, pp. 29–61

45 Germaine Greer, *The Female Eunuch*, as above, p. 131

46 John Kremer and Jenny Marks, as above, pp. 5–15

47 *Working Women*, [GMB magazine], winter 1992, p. 15
48 *The Sunday Times*, 25 June 1989
49 Ronald Hyam, *Empire and Sexuality*, as above, p. 72
50 Statistics from the UN Decade for Women
51 Simone de Beauvoir, *The Second Sex* (first pub. 1949; London, Picador, 1988), pp. 23–4
52 Michael Asher, *Shoot to Kill* (London, Viking, 1990), pp. 153–4
53 Andrew Tolson, *The Limits of Masculinity*, as above, pp. 59–60
54 Sergeant Rona Anderson and others, as above, p. 86
55 Simone de Beauvoir, *The Second Sex*, as above, p. 24
56 *The Daily Express*, 6 January 1993
57 *The Guardian*, 23 February 1993
58 'Persistence of men's misperceptions of friendly cues across a variety of interpersonal encounters', *Psychology of Women Quarterly*, no. 15, 1991, pp. 463–75
59 *Working Women*, [GMB paper], winter 1992
60 Michael Rubenstein, *Preventing and Remedying Sexual Harassment at Work* (London, Industrial Relations Services, 1989), p. 26
61 Naomi Wolf, *The Beauty Myth* (London, Vintage, 1991), pp. 152, 158
62 *The Guardian*, 26–27 October 1991
63 Quoted in *The Guardian*, 7 January 1993
64 Naomi Wolf, *The Beauty Myth*, as above, p. 273
65 *Bella*, 10 September 1988
66 ACTT report on sexual harassment
67 *Working Women*, [GMB magazine], winter 1992
68 COHSE survey, 1991
69 ACTT report on sexual harassment
70 ACTT report on sexual harassment
71 Sergeant Rona Anderson and others, as above, 1993
72 *The Guardian*, 23 January 1993
73 *The Independent*, 4 December 1992
74 Article by Alice Leonard, *New Law Journal*, 8 November 1991, pp. 1514–16
75 *Hansard*, House of Lords, 30 March 1993, Cols 817–24
76 Article by Alice Leonard, as above
77 *The Independent*, 15 March 1989

Index

CREDITS: *The Beauty Myth*, Naomi Wolf, Chatto & Windus/ Hutchinson; *Changing Social Work and Welfare*, Cater, Jeffs, Smiths, Open University Press; Clancy Sigal's article, 'Hollywood Diary' in *The Guardian* (14.11.91); *Dear Clare . . .* , Clare Short, editors: Diane Hutchinson, Kiri Tunks, Hutchinson Radius; *Empire and Sexuality*, Ronald Hyam, Manchester University Press; *The Female Eunuch*, Germaine Greer, HarperCollins Publishers Ltd; Laurie Taylor's article in *The Times* (18.10.91); *The Limits of Masculinity*, Andrew Toulson, Tavistock Publications; *The Second Sex*, Simone de Beauvoir, translator: H. M. Parshley, Jonathan Cape; *Sexual Harassment: Women Speak Out*, introduction by Amber Coverdall Sumrall and Dena Taylor, The Crossing Press, California; *Shoot to Kill*, Michael Asher, Penguin Books, by kind permission of David Higham Associates; *Stability and Flexibility in Hadza Residential Groupings*, James Woodburn, Aldine Publishing, Chicago.